Forensic Perspectives on Cybercrime

Forensic Perspectives on Cybercrime is the first book to combine the disciplines of cyberpsychology and forensic psychology, helping to define this emergent area. It explores the psychological factors that influence the behaviour of all those involved in cybersecurity, drawing upon the research literatures in relevant areas including forensic, social, and cyberpsychology.

Written by leading figures in the field, the book provides an introduction to the cybercrime ecosystem, before discussing the psychological manipulation of targets through social engineering techniques and highlighting the unique threats that this type of attack presents. The reasons why people become involved in hacking are explored, and the authors review research literature on risk factors of being a victim of cybercrime, along with the concept of resilience. Behaviour change and prevention strategies are also evaluated, as well as the role of emergent technologies such as artificial intelligence and what this may mean for the role of humans in cybersecurity. Case studies and real-world examples are woven throughout to illustrate key issues, opportunities, and challenges.

This unique text is a must-read for students undertaking any degree that relates to behaviour and cybersecurity, including psychology, computing, law, and business management. It is also highly relevant to researchers, practitioners, and policymakers who work in cybersecurity and/or have an interest in empowering people to be safe online.

John McAlaney is a Chartered Psychologist and Chartered Scientist at Bournemouth University. His research looks at psychological determinants of risk behaviours including online gambling, digital addiction, and cybersecurity. He engages with charities, businesses, and policymakers to help them empower individuals to protect themselves and others from online harms.

Peter J. Hills is a Cognitive Psychologist by training who has published over 60 peer-reviewed research articles using various experimental and non-experimental methods to research aspects of psychology relevant to the forensic domain including face recognition, sexual violence reduction, and online/offline misogyny and sexism.

Terri Cole worked for the National Crime Agency providing behavioural investigative advice to serious crime investigations for many years. She currently works at Bournemouth University lecturing and researching how psychological knowledge can be applied to crime investigations. She has previously authored two books including a BPS textbook of the year.

New Frontiers in Forensic Psychology

Series Editors

Graham Towl is Professor of Forensic Psychology at Durham University and was formerly Chief Psychologist at the Ministry of Justice, UK. He is the recipient of the British Psychological Society Awards for Distinguished Contributions to Professional Practice and forensic academic knowledge.

Tammi Walker is Professor of Forensic Psychology and Principal of St Cuthbert's Society Durham University. She is a Chartered Psychologist and Fellow of the British Psychological Society. Her research interests are gendered interventions for managing self-harm and suicide in prisons, mental health, physical health and addressing sexual violence in universities.

New Frontiers in Forensic Psychology is a new series of forensic psychology books, which brings together the most contemporary research in core and emerging topics in the field, providing a comprehensive review of new areas of investigation in forensic psychology, and new perspectives on existing topics of enquiry. The series includes original volumes in which the authors are encouraged to explore unchartered territory, make cross-disciplinary evaluations, and where possible break new ground. The series is an essential resource for senior undergraduates, postgraduates, researchers and practitioners across forensic psychology, criminology, and social policy.

New Perspectives on Arson and Firesetting
The Human-Fire Use Relationship
Faye K. Horsley

Risk Assessment in Forensic Practice
David Crighton

Forensic Perspectives on Cybercrime
Human Behaviour and Cybersecurity
John McAlaney, Peter J. Hills, and Terri Coles

For a complete list of all books in this series, please visit the series page at: https://www.routledge.com/New-Frontiers-in-Forensic-Psychology/book-series/NFFP

Forensic Perspectives on Cybercrime

Human Behaviour and Cybersecurity

JOHN McALANEY, PETER J. HILLS, AND TERRI COLE

Routledge
Taylor & Francis Group

LONDON AND NEW YORK

Designed cover image: © Getty images

First published 2024
by Routledge
4 Park Square, Milton Park, Abingdon, Oxon OX14 4RN

and by Routledge
605 Third Avenue, New York, NY 10158

Routledge is an imprint of the Taylor & Francis Group, an informa business

© 2024 John McAlaney, Peter J. Hills, and Terri Cole

British Library Cataloguing-in-Publication Data
A catalogue record for this book is available from the British Library

Library of Congress Cataloging-in-Publication Data
Names: McAlaney, John, 1979- author. | Hills, Peter J. (Lecturer), author. |
Cole, Terri, author.
Title: Forensic perspectives on cybercrime : human behaviour and cybersecurity /
John McAlaney, Peter J. Hills and Terri Cole.
Description: Abingdon, Oxon ; New York, NY : Routledge, 2024. | Includes
bibliographical references and index. |
Identifiers: LCCN 2023041491 (print) | LCCN 2023041492 (ebook) |
ISBN 9781032291758 (hardback) | ISBN 9781032291741 (paperback) |
ISBN 9781003300359 (ebook)
Subjects: LCSH: Computer crimes—Psychological aspects. | Computer
crimes—Social aspects. | Computer security. | Forensic psychology. | Criminology.
Classification: LCC HV6773 .M3839 2024 (print) | LCC HV6773 (ebook) |
DDC 364.16/8—dc23/eng/20231212
LC record available at https://lccn.loc.gov/2023041491
LC ebook record available at https://lccn.loc.gov/2023041492

ISBN: 978-1-032-29175-8 (hbk)
ISBN: 978-1-032-29174-1 (pbk)
ISBN: 978-1-003-30035-9 (ebk)

DOI: 10.4324/9781003300359

Typeset in Avenir and Dante
by codeMantra

John McAlaney – *To all of the ethical hackers and social engineers out there who seek to change things for the better.*

Peter J. Hills – *As with all areas of my life, I dedicate this to my adorable, and very cheeky, son, Arthur, and my lovely, and very smart, wife, Sarah.*

Terri Cole – *To Lily and Alfie. My absolute world. Both on and offline.*

Contents

Series Foreword

We are delighted to introduce the new book by Professor John McAlaney, Dr Terri Cole, and Professor Peter J. Hills entitled *Forensic Perspectives on Cybercrime* for our New Frontiers in Forensic Psychology series. This book explores the psychological factors that influence the behaviour of all those involved in cybersecurity, drawing upon the research literatures in relevant areas including forensic, social, and cyber psychology.

Computers and the internet are used in almost every field of human society either in homes, schools, colleges, factories, or businesses. These digital technologies provide many benefits to individuals and organisations; however, they also facilitate criminal activities. Cybercrimes take place online and take place over electronic communications or information systems. This book begins with an introduction on the rapidly evolving ecosystem of cybercrime. It then moves onto discussing the social engineering processes that are used to *psychologically manipulate people to make security mistakes or* give away sensitive information. The motives for why individuals become involved in hacking are explored and a review is presented of the results from the research literature on risk factors of being a victim of cybercrime, along with the concept of resilience. National and organisational culture are considered in relation to how cyber attackers may seek to exploit these factors. Behaviour change and prevention strategies are appraised within the context of the online environment. Lastly, the role of emergent technologies such as eye tracking and artificial intelligence in relation to cybersecurity is considered.

New Frontiers in Forensic Psychology brings together the most contemporary research in core and emerging topics in the field, providing a comprehensive review of new areas of investigation in forensic psychology and new perspectives on existing topics of enquiry.

The series includes original volumes in which the authors are encouraged to explore unchartered territory, make cross-disciplinary evaluations and, where possible, break new ground.

The series is an essential resource for senior undergraduates, postgraduates, researchers, and practitioners across forensic psychology, criminology, and social policy.

The authors are donating the royalties in full to STARS Dorset.
Professor Tammi Walker and Professor Graham Towl
Series Editors
Department of Psychology, Durham University

Introduction to cybercrime 1

Context

We live in an increasingly inter-connected world. The digital technologies that underpin these societal changes provide many benefits to individuals and organisations, however they also facilitate criminal activities. There is enhanced public awareness of the real-world impact of cybersecurity incidents, in part due to high profile cases such as the WannaCry ransomware worm that had a large impact on the National Health Service (NHS) in the UK (BBC News, 2017). In 2022, the data of 400 million Twitter users was stolen, which included email addresses and phone numbers linked to accounts, information which could be used or sold to cybercriminals to facilitate further breaches (Newman, 2023). Data breaches of this type can also result in the real-life identity of people being revealed, which for some individuals may be harmful if they make use of a pseudonym online to protect their identity. In addition, cyber-attacks increasingly impact on the daily lives of members of the public, such as in the ransomware attack on the Colonial Pipeline in 2021. This is an oil pipeline system that transports gasoline and jet fuel from Texas in the USA to the southeast of the country. Due to the cyber-attack, the company ceased all operations of the pipeline, resulting in fuel shortages, panic buying, and changes to flight schedules. This led U.S. President Joe Biden to declare a state of emergency, with the Colonial Pipeline Company paying the attackers 75 Bitcoin ($4.4 million) to regain access to their systems (Kerner, 2022).

Psychological factors underlie the cognitions and behaviours of all the actors within cybersecurity. This includes the decision-making process that leads the attackers to choose their targets; and then the choice of methods used in the

DOI: 10.4324/9781003300359-1

attack. This has parallels with the decision-making processes identified in forensic psychology with reference to offline crimes, such as the processes used by burglars to decide which house to burgle (Nee & Meenaghan, 2020). These decisions may be influenced by the perceptions that the attackers have of how the targets will respond to the attack. More broadly, cybersecurity incidents may change how the wider public interacts with online technologies, such as their trust in online voting systems or engagement with online shopping.

In this opening chapter we outline this cybercrime landscape, with a focus on the theories from forensic, cyber, social, and other areas of psychology that can help us understand the behaviours and cognitions of all of those involved in cybercrime. Everyday use of technology involves basic interactions that reflect social processes. Passwords for example have been described as trusted tokens (Marshall & Stephens, 2008), in which individuals provide proof of their identity in exchange for access to services. However, such interactions are prone to the same compromises that people make in other aspects of their daily lives so that they are able to navigate a complex social world with finite resources. Tam, Glassman, and Vandenwauver (2010) for instance note the convenience-security trade-off, in which people opt for simpler passwords than would be recommended by security experts, as it is often challenging for people to choose and recall more complex passwords. This is consistent with rational choice theory, in which individuals decide on what action to take based on their judgement of the costs and benefits of each action (Ostrom, 1998). This tendency is the reason behind passwords being required to have a certain level of complexity, such as for example the mandate that a password must include a capital letter, number, special character etc. Whilst setting such a requirement may feel intuitive from a cybersecurity perspective it can create issues for the humans who are the users of socio-technological systems. A recurrent theme throughout this book will be the clash between how humans should ideally behave to avoid cyber-risks versus the actual, less than ideal cybersecurity behaviours that humans often exhibit.

A challenge in understanding human behaviour in online settings is whether people behave in a fundamentally different way online, or if online technologies just provide them the opportunity to express themselves in ways that would not otherwise be possible. This relates to the question put forward by Suler (2004) on whether the internet transforms or enhances. An example would be whether someone who behaves aggressively in an online interaction would also do so if they were having a similar interaction offline (i.e., if the online setting transforms that behaviour), or if the online setting just exaggerates how aggressively that person behaves (i.e., if it enhances an existing behaviour). This is in turn linked to the concept of digital drift. This refers to how technology can lead individuals to loosen their adherence to mainstream norms (Brewer, Fox, & Miller, 2019). This can happen in the digital context by providing affinity (i.e., financial and social rewards) and affiliation (i.e., associating with others). Goldsmith and Brewer (2015) argue that people can take advantage of the internet to express different online identities and to escape into a virtual world with less conforming social norms. This theme of existing outside of mainstream society and creating a new or curated identity is certainly something that would appear to be evident in the conversations that have been reported to take place between members of hacking groups, as documented by several authors (Coleman, 2014; Olson, 2012).

The pervasiveness of online technologies in the lives of many of us facilitates the actions of cybercriminals. In the UK, most people (62%) have up to nine online accounts (including social media platforms, online banking, online shopping etc.) that contain sensitive data, with more than a third (38%) having ten or more (CybSafe, 2022). In addition, individuals often have access to sensitive data of others through computer systems in their workplaces. This is one of the reasons why many cybersecurity breaches of organisations have been found to be a result of human error, typically due to a social engineering attack (CybSafe, 2022) of the types that are discussed in Chapter 2. The importance of understanding human factors is recognised as a key aspect of cybersecurity by cybersecurity experts and practitioners (Kearney & Kruger, 2016). However, as will be explored in later chapters, there often exists a perception of humans as the 'weak link' of cybersecurity. This is potentially a harmful belief as it creates an expectation for all stakeholders in cybersecurity – the targets, the attackers, and the IT professionals that seek to protect systems – that it is the users who are the point of failure. This may lead to several unintended consequences, such as learned helplessness of the type documented throughout psychological research (Abramson, Seligman, & Teasdale, 1978), where individuals come to believe that there is nothing they can do to prevent a negative situation from arising. This reflects the common message used by cybersecurity professionals that it is not a question of if you get hacked, but when. The rationale behind this message is presumably to encourage potential victims to be more vigilant and overcome any complacency they hold about cyber-risks. It is understandable perhaps that it is felt that there is a need to emphasise the risks. Throughout this book examples will be given of how large, well-resourced companies, including technology companies, have been breached using often surprisingly simple social engineering attacks and hacking techniques. Nevertheless, it must be considered that this narrative of humans being the weak link and cyber-attacks as inescapable maybe counter-productive and self-fulfilling by leading some to believe that whatever they do can be hacked, so it is pointless to even try to avoid this.

A successful hack enables the attackers to engage in other activities beyond the theft of sensitive data. This includes website defacement, interference with the lawful use of computers, and the dissemination of malicious software

(Grabosky, 2016). Hacking can also be used to create botnets, in which other devices are hijacked – typically without the knowledge of the owners – and used to commit further acts of hacking (Kremling & Parker, 2017). This can include Distributed Denial of Service (DDoS) attacks, in which websites and other online services are taken offline by being inundated with connection requests. The scale of cybercrime can be difficult to envisage. Much of the work of cyber-criminals involves the use of software to facilitate their goals. For example, 80 billion automated scans are made daily by cybercriminals, aimed at identifying vulnerable targets (Lewis, 2018). The increase in cybercrime in recent decades (Furnell, Emm, & Papadaki, 2015) contrasts with the decrease globally since the 1990s in offline crime (Tseloni, Mailley, Farrell, & Tilley, 2010). In addition, as will be discussed in Chapter 3, the range of potential suspects in cybercrime can be more varied than can be the case with offline crime. As a basic example, any interpersonal crime such as an assault needs an offender and victim to be in the same location in terms of time and space. Suspects are therefore limited to individuals who could feasibly have been in the physical location of the crime at the time it occurred. Cybercrime however can be committed by a substantially larger pool of suspects, who could be located nearly anywhere in the world. For example, a 10 year old boy was rewarded with $10,000 after finding a major security flaw in Instagram (Lee, 2016). Similarly, as will be discussed in Chapter 4, there are inconsistent results in the research literature on who the most likely victims of cybercrime are.

As with any behaviour, the actions of all of those involved in a cybersecurity incident can be influenced by the cultures in which those individuals exist. This can relate to both the culture of the organisation that an individual is part of, and the national cultures that all or parts of the organisations operate in. Within the UK, the most common identified threat vector are phishing attacks, as identified in a report by the Department of Culture Media and Sport (2022). Whether or not an employee clicks on a malicious link or attachment in a phishing email will be determined by several national organisational and cultural factors, including their perception of risk and perceptions of expected productivity (i.e., the speed at which emails should be processed). This report also found that 54% of businesses have acted in the previous 12 months to identify cybersecurity risks, although qualitative interviews found that limited understanding at the board level led to responsibility being passed onto external providers or internal colleagues. This is an issue, as the management of a company set the tone for how all employees respond to potential cyber threats. These cybersecurity culture factors represent a complex challenge in how to change risk behaviours in an organisation, as discussed in Chapter 5.

Given the role of human behaviour and cognition in cybersecurity incidents there has been an increasing recognition of the importance of applying behaviour change and prevention strategies. The online environment creates unique opportunities to encourage people to change their behaviour, but also adds novel challenges. Many online actions, such as for example an employee's use of a work computer in an organisation, can be monitored, and recorded. This can provide insights into the factors that may lead to an employee becoming a victim of cybercrime. The same technology can be used to deliver personalised, data-driven behaviour change and prevention strategies. Yet as will be discussed in Chapter 6 there are many examples through the psychological research literature of such campaigns in other domains that have been ineffectual or counterproductive. As such, there is need for evidence-based techniques to be used to promote behaviour change and prevention of cybercrime, which also reflects the differences between online and offline crime.

More recently, advances in big data, machine learning, and artificial intelligence (AI) have been exploited by both those who seek to commit cybercrime and those who strive to prevent it. For example, the amount of personal data produced by online technologies is extensive, with Facebook alone generating the equivalent of over 2,000 billion pages of printed text every day in 2019 (Brandwatch, 2019). This wealth of data potentially provides cybercriminals and cybersecurity experts with new means with which to achieve their goals. A challenge of big data however is that it is more extensive than can be analysed using conventional means. This is where machine learning and artificial intelligence are increasingly utilised, including within cybersecurity. One potential promise of AI is the ability for unbiased decision making to be made, which would potentially be very useful when combatting social engineering attacks. However it has been demonstrated that human biases can still be evident in the machine learning and AI technologies that have been used in cybersecurity (Lima & Keegan, 2020). The implications and questions caused by these emergent technologies are explored in Chapter 7.

An ongoing challenge in cybersecurity is that technology can, by design, be set up in a way that is intended to make the user as anonymous as possible. For example, the dark web consists of internet sites that cannot be accessed through standard web browsers. The dark web is something which people often have an awareness but struggle to fully visualise. This can partly be due to conflation between the dark web and the deep web. The deep web refers to information that is available in an online format, but which is not indexed by the web crawlers used by popular search engines. An example of deep web data would include information such as student records at a university. Such information is online and accessible to relevant staff and students through the intranet of the organisation, but this information cannot be located simply by searching on Google. The dark web on the other hand refers to a section of the deep web that is deliberately hidden and which can only be accessed with online tools. Both the deep web and the dark web lie beneath the surface web, which could be described as the normal, everyday internet that most people are familiar with. One of the most well-known tools used to access the dark web is The Onion Router (Tor), which provides a web browser through which dark web sites can be accessed. Despite the negative connotations often associated with Tor and use of the dark web in general it is important to note that use of Tor is not illegal. Indeed, the software was developed by the United States Naval Research Laboratory, for the purpose of protecting online American intelligence communications (Lawrence, 2014). The software is used for many purposes beyond what would be considered criminal activity, such as for example by journalists reporting from oppressive regimes who wish to protect themselves (Bartlett, 2014). Nevertheless, the dark web has garnered a near-mythical status of being a lawless and sinister online space where any act of depravity can be found. It is the case however that the dark web and Tor have been used to disseminate extreme materials such as child pornography, likely in the belief by those creating and sharing such materials that the technology reduces their risk of being identified.

The cybercrime ecosystem revolves around money. Increasingly, these financial transactions make use of cryptocurrencies, another technology that has arisen from the internet. This is a type of digital currency that uses cryptography techniques to ensure secure and easily verifiable financial transactions. In contrast to mainstream, traditional banking, cryptocurrencies are decentralised. That is, there is no single agency or organisation that manages the cryptocurrency. This lack of regulation and centralisation has prompted varying reactions from governments across the world. For example, it has been suggested that the US administration is actively seeking to suppress the use of cryptocurrencies in the USA (Reynolds, 2023). Cryptocurrencies operate through a technology called the blockchain, which uses a distributed ledger in which all transactions are recorded across multiple computers, or nodes. The first widely used cryptocurrency was Bitcoin, which was created in 2009. Since then, other cryptocurrencies have been created, known as altcoins. Examples of these include Ethereum and Litecoin. Cryptocurrencies are traded through cryptocurrency exchanges, often referred to as bitcoin exchanges, where users can trade their cryptocurrency tokens for other digital currencies, or for conventional currencies. These cryptocurrencies have several benefits, including faster and cheaper cross-country transactions, as well providing access to financial services for people who do not have a bank account. Given the lack of any central regulation or oversight, it is not surprising that cryptocurrencies have become a popular technology with cybercriminals. More broadly, they appeal to the wider hacker culture that places value on people finding new ways to do things – in this case a financial system that does not include the various issues, controversies and unethical business practices found in traditional banking. Cryptocurrencies also provide opportunities for individuals to make profit through the same means seen in traditional financial systems, such as arbitrage, in which someone can take advantage of prices differences across markets to make money (Kabasinskas & Sutiene, 2021).

However, cryptocurrencies do not necessarily provide the level of security and privacy that some cryptocurrency users may hope. In *Tracers in the Dark: The Global Hunt for the Crime Lords of Cryptocurrency*, Greenberg (2022) identifies some of the misperceptions that are held about cryptocurrencies. Despite being seen by users of the technology as anonymous, the nature of the blockchain is that every transaction is recorded. Whilst the offline identity of those behind cryptocurrency may not be immediately apparent, there are numerous examples where law enforcement has successfully identified individuals who have used cryptocurrency for criminal means. In addition, there have been cases of cryptocurrency exchanges being hacked, or the people behind the cryptocurrency absconding with the money. An example of this was Mt. Gox, a cryptocurrency exchange that at one point processed over 70% of all Bitcoin transactions worldwide. It suddenly ceased trading in 2014, with cryptocurrency the equivalent of hundreds of millions of US dollars unavailable to the owners of those tokens, equating to 7% of all bitcoins in existence at the time. The CEO of Mt. Gox, a then 30 year old named Mark Karpeles, was arrested and charged with fraud and embezzlement by Japanese police. He was later acquitted of these crimes, although the verdict noted that he had inflicted extensive harm on the trust of his users. In *The Missing Cryptoqueen: The Billion Dollar Cryptocurrency Con and the Woman Who Got Away With It,* Jamie Bartlett describes the case of Ruja Ignatova (Bartlett, 2022), who is the founder of a fraudulent cryptocurrency scheme called OneCoin. This cryptocurrency was a new manifestation of an old scam, namely a pyramid scheme. In contrast to other cryptocurrencies, OneCoin used a centralised model rather than a decentralised one. The company used multi-level marketing tactics to attract new investors by promising high returns and offering commission to those who recruited others to join the scheme. These cases demonstrate the ingenuity with which cybercriminals can find ways to exploit new technologies.

Types of cybercrime

There are many different types of cybercrime, and many different cybercriminal actions. The Crown Prosecution Service in the UK makes a distinction between cyber-dependent crimes and cyber-enabled crimes (Crown Prosecution Service, 2023). Cyber-dependent crimes are those that can only be committed using information technologies (IT), which includes the creation and dissemination of malware for financial gain, and hacking to steal, damage, or distort data and networks. Cyber-enabled crimes on the other hand are traditional crimes that can be increased through IT, which includes acts of fraud, online marketplaces for illicit items, and the grooming of children by online sexual predators. This boundary between cyber-dependent and cyber-enabled crimes is helpful in understanding cybercrime but can though be blurred. This reflects the increasing pervasiveness of internet technologies in daily life. The distinction between online and offline activities is no longer as clear as it once was.

Increasingly, technological devices can make remote connections through the internet or other means, which creates new opportunities for cybercriminals that go beyond the stereotypical act of stealing bank account details. The inter-connected nature of socio-technical systems means that a cyber-attack can have multiple offline impacts. For example, hackers have been able to hack cars (Kelion, 2016) and caused gridlock in Moscow by hacking a taxi system (Holroyd, 2022), and in 2016 the internet of Liberia crashed after a cybercriminal attacked an African phone company (Casciani, 2017). The internet can also be used for the purchase of illicit materials such as drugs. This highlights the differing attitudes that can exist when a crime is committed online as opposed to offline, and the overlap that can exist between the two. For instance, an investigation by the BBC reported the perceived ease of purchasing illicit drugs online, including through the dark web. The report also noted the views of postal workers that attempting to prevent this practice was largely futile (Connolly & Doble, 2017). Examples such as this raise interesting but challenging questions on how we, as a society, decide what forms of cybercrime we can and should prioritise for prevention and mitigation strategies, allowing for the fact that there are finite resources with which to support these strategies.

In the text below we explore some of the broad categories of cybercrime, with the caveat that there is overlap between many of these activities.

Hacking

Hacking is the single activity that is perhaps most associated with cybercrime. The term 'hacking' invokes the Hollywood imagery of a figure in a black hoodie, sitting in front of a computer monitor in a dark room whilst lines of programming code scroll across the screen. It is a phenomenon that has been defined in multiple ways, often with negative connotations that conflate hacking with criminality. For instance, hacking has been defined as unauthorised access of a computer system with criminal intent (Grabosky, 2016). In turn, the term 'hacker' has evolved to encompass more than the act of hacking itself. Maimon and Louderback (2019) argue that hacking is distinct from cyber-trespassing, defined as crossing of the invisible boundaries of online environments (Walls, 2001), with hacking encompassing a wider range of behaviour and participation in hacker culture. This hacker culture is evident in both online and offline spaces, such as the DEF CON events that take place in Las Vegas each summer (defcon.org). The event regularly attracts in excess of 20,000 attendees (DEF CON, 2023), and provides a rich and varied programme of talks, demonstrations, discussions, and social activities. This and the similar events that take place across the world highlight that communities of hackers go beyond the popular conceptions of hacking as a niche activity conducted by malcontents, sitting in a dark room. Indeed, many of the activities undertaken in hacking culture could be argued to directly benefit society. A regular exercise at the annual DEF CON event is publicly demonstrating how devices that are thought – or at least hoped – to be secure can be breached, including secure access systems and electronic voting machines. Highlighting security vulnerabilities on the stage in a large ballroom in Las Vegas may not seem like a socially responsible activity, but these activities provide an impetus for companies to ensure that their products are as secure as possible. Similarly, there are individuals who work as ethical hackers. These individuals are employed by organisations to conduct penetration testing, in which they will test the cybersecurity of an organisation by attempting to breach that cybersecurity. Further discussion of this type of hacking is given in Chapter 3.

It has been observed that successful hacking requires a series of consecutive activities (Steinmetz, 2014), which includes gathering preliminary intelligence on the technical and social characteristics of their targets, exploiting the identified vulnerabilities, the elevation of privileges (increasing access to data), and then the attempt to cover up evidence of their hack. Maimon and Louderback (2019) argue that hacking is considered as the starting point for most types of cyber-dependent crimes. Hacking does not in itself however necessarily require extensive skills or technological knowledge. For example, script kiddies, which refer to individuals who make use of software tools to perform hacking acts, may have little technical ability but can still cause widespread disruption. In one case 34 individuals, many of them teenagers, were arrested from 13 different countries as part of an operation investigating the Netspoof DDoS attack tool. This online service enabled paying users to deploy DDoS-for-hire software and launch cyber-attacks (Khandelwal, 2016). As outlined above, a DDoS attach (distributed denial of service) can cause a website or online service to cease to function by overwhelming that website or service with requests – akin to repeatedly pressing the refresh button on a page of a web browser, but with millions of requests per second. This is often facilitated using botnets, of the type discussed earlier in this chapter. This act of hacking is effective, perhaps because it is such a crude tool. Nevertheless, it is one that can be effective, especially when the goal is to cause disruption to an organisation. This demonstrates another key theme of the book – that hacking is not limited to motivations of financial gain. As will be discussed in Chapter 3, there are varied motivations for engaging in hacking, including hacktivism where the main goal is ideological in nature.

Scams

Cybercrimes reflect offline crimes, especially those with a financial element such as scams. One of the most common approaches used are phishing emails, which can include several elements such as links or files that, if opened, will install malicious software on a computer system. Alternatively, phishing emails or online messages may be used to establish a personal relationship with the target for the purposes of coercion later, such as in the case of romance scams. Many of us will have experience of receiving an email that is easily identifiable as a phishing one due to its dubious claims (such as a lottery win) and grammatical errors, but phishing emails have become substantially more sophisticated and tailored since their earlier iterations (Nurse, 2015). Iuga, Nurse, and Erola (2016) note that technological solutions to preventing the harms associated with phishing emails are useful but limited, emphasising the need for better understanding of the human element of phishing emails. Phishing can also take place through malicious websites. Fake Facebook groups have been used to scam individuals, such as a group page named the Total Wipeout Tour that presented itself as being associated with the TV show, albeit with a non-descript statement confirming that this was not the case (BBC News, 2016). Individuals who wished to participate in this fictitious tour were asked to complete forms that requested their email address, date of birth and Facebook profile. No financial or banking details were requested. As such it may be that people who engaged with these pages did not perceive there to be any threat, which would be as predicted by Protection Motivation Theory (Rogers, 1975). However, a threat is still present. Information provided to pages such as this one could be a case of data mining, in which the information collected is sold to marketing companies. In addition, the page may prompt individuals to share and like it, gathering users until it is then sold to a business and undergoes a name change. This creates a deception in which a company is perceived to have a better reputation than would otherwise be the case.

Cyberbullying and online harassment

Cyberbullying refers to the act of bullying through electronic means, although as Zhu, Huang, Evans, and Zhang (2021) note it is a relatively new field of research. A contributing factor to cyberbullying may be that children and adolescents struggle to understand the connection between behaviours and consequences (Agatston & Limber, 2018), something which may be exacerbated by the online disinhibition effect (Suler, 2004). This refers to the feeling that individuals may have that online interactions are not as real as offline interactions. Despite this, it has been suggested that the impact of cyberbullying can be greater than offline bullying, as the preparators can access the victim anonymously, at any time of day and from any geographical location (Hutson, Kelly, & Militello, 2018). The impact of cyberbullying can be extensive on those who are targeted, and can include depression, anxiety, emotional distress, suicidal ideation and self-harm, somatic complaints, reduced physical health, absenteeism, self-esteem problems, increased delinquency, and increased substance use (Vaillancourt, Faris, & Mishna, 2017). Whether or not cyberbullying is a crime is something that varies by country. In the UK for instance there are no specific laws that cover cyberbullying. Instead, any offences that are prosecuted must draw upon more generic and often outdated laws, such as the Communication Act 2003 which prohibits the sending of messages that are 'grossly offensive or of an indecent, obscene or menacing character'. A further legal complication is that the perpetrators of cyberbullying may be especially likely to be minors, although of course adults can be both the instigators and target of cyberbullying as well. It has been suggested that the move towards online teaching during the COVID-19 pandemic created additional cyberbullying risks as teachers often had less direct control over their classrooms, and that the use of webcams gave cyberbullies greater opportunities to take images of their targets for aggressive purposes (Halder, 2022).

Other forms of online harassment exist which, as with cyberbullying, often consist of using technology to facilitate harmful actions that also take place offline. An example of this comes from the group who are known as incels. This originates from 'involuntary celibate' and refers to individuals – primarily male – who consider themselves unable to find a romantic or sexual partners, despite the desire for one. The incel phenomenon is documented by Lisa Sugiura in *The Incel Rebellion: The Rise of the Manosphere and the Virtual War Against Women* (Sugiura, 2021), which notes the many and varied misogynistic acts, online and offline, that are committed against women. High profile examples include the case of Jake Davison, who shot and killed five people in Plymouth, UK, in August 2021. Media reports at the time stated that Davison was motivated by incel ideology that he encountered online, and the 'heroes' of the movement who advocate violence against women (Morris, 2021).

Crime as a service

The provision of hacking tools and other types of malware cybercriminals for financial gain has been labelled Crimeware-as-a-Service (CaaS). The cybercriminals sell their expertise, knowledge, and access to specialist tools to those who do not have the ability or inclination to commit cybercrimes themselves. This business model is not fundamentally different from other 'as-a-service' (AAS) models that are used extensively throughout legitimate businesses, such as software as a service where a company does not directly own the software it uses, but instead uses software provided by an external company. The benefits of using the AAS approach is the same for cybercriminals as it is for legitimate business. Barriers to entry are removed, individuals can focus on the core activities and goals, and – even in cybercriminal examples – access to customer support can be available. A cursory visit to the dark web via Tor will enable someone to find many adverts that list services such as hacking of social media accounts, DDoSing of nominated targets or the changing of school or university grades. It should be noted though that amongst hackers and cybercriminals there is a perception that many of these services on offer are themselves a scam (Bartlett, 2014).

CaaS has been argued to be largely invisible to governments and law enforcement agencies (An & Kim, 2018). A distinction has been made between CaaS and crimeware, with the former described as a do-it-for-me service, and the latter described as a do-it-yourself product (An & Kim, 2018). It has similarly been noted that there is a lack of research into CaaS (An & Kim, 2018), perhaps not surprising given the methodological challenges and ethical considerations involved in accessing these networks. Nevertheless, a better understanding of CaaS is needed. These services are a key component of the cybercriminal ecosystem, and as such knowing how to disrupt CaaS activities has the potential to create barriers for actors operating in that cybercriminal ecosystem. The role of CaaS in the cybercrime ecosystem is discussed in further detail in Chapter 3.

Cybercriminal ecosystems

A cybercriminal business ecosystem has evolved over time, as individuals realised that their skills around programming, marketing, and the development of technology platforms could be commercialised (Holt, 2007). It has been commented that this business model is in fact a highly professional one (An & Kim, 2018). Sood and Enbody (2013) argue that there are three key elements in a cybercrime marketplace – actors, value chains, and modes of operation. An and Kim (2018) make a distinction between two types of products or service that are available in the cybercrime underground, although they note that definitions and conceptualisations of CaaS vary in the literature. The first of these are products or services that relate to attack strategies. This includes phishing, brute force attacks, DDoS attacks, and ransomware. The second type of attack involves targeting and neutralising the preventative measures used by organisations, such as firewalls or anti-virus software. It is interesting to note that social engineering products and services – that is attacks based on psychological manipulation – appear to be rarely traded on underground cybercriminal networks (An & Kim, 2018).

As noted, cybercriminal gangs make use of hacking tools that can be purchased on cybercrime black markets. There has been a move within cybercrime from being product-orientated to service orientated, although the different temporal and spatial characteristics of the online space creates challenges in making comparisons to traditional, legitimate business models (An & Kim, 2018). As such cybercriminals are highly dependent on closed underground communities such as Hackforums and Crackingzilla. It has been observed that the anonymity that is available in these cybercrime networks results in different group structures than are observed in offline criminal networks, such as the Mafia (Brenner, 2003). Whilst traditional crime structures are vertical, concentrated, rigid, and fixed, cybercriminal group structures are more lateral, fluid, diffuse, and evolve more rapidly (An & Kim, 2018). In addition, the popularity of different products and services changes over time (An & Kim, 2018). Monitoring of these marketplaces provides opportunities for threat intelligence and prevention strategies. As with offline criminal networks, these market places have on occasion been infiltrated by law enforcement agents, with a view to shutting them down (Chen, Chiang, & Storey, 2012). This reflects the broader cybercrime ecosystem, which has been proposed to consist of cyber criminals, enablers (those who support the online criminal operations), guardians (law enforcement and IT professionals who strive to protect systems), and targets (Kraemer-Mbula, Tang, & Rush, 2013).

McGuire (2012) makes a distinction between disorganised groups of cyber criminals that communicate online but have no clear chain of command (the swarm structure) and organised groups with a clear organisational hierarchy (the hub structure). Hackers also have different levels of socialisation, from small and intimate peer networks to the broader community of hackers (Macdonald & Frank, 2017). Individuals who share information with others are central to both groups (Holt, Bossler, & May, 2012), which is one of the ways in which novice hackers learn new skills (Décary-Hétu & Dupont, 2012). Choo and Smith (2008) further argue there are three types of cybercrime groups:

- Traditional organised criminals
  - Using crime as a service (CaaS) models
- Organised cybercriminal groups (for example groups such as LulzSec)
  - Distinguished from the previous type by members having shared goals and communicating with each other, but without necessarily revealing their identity
- Ideologically and politically motivated groups (for example Anonymous)
  - Groups who engage in hacktivism and who may commit crimes, but who are not necessarily criminally motivated

Group structures and processes are discussed in more detail in Chapter 3.

Huang, Guo, Guo, and Li (2021) have demonstrated that it is possible to identify key hackers on underground forums using a tool called HackerRank, that utilises automated social network analysis and content analysis. It could be argued that this shows a greater ease in identifying hackers on underground forums than those hackers may realise.

Cyberwarfare and fake news

Cyberwarfare broadly refers to the use of internet technologies to cause harm and disruption against a nation state, although it has been noted that definitions of this phenomenon vary (Wilcox, 2018). One of the first examples of an act of cyberwarfare was the Stuxnet incident (Atrews, 2020), in which a computer worm (a type of malicious software) caused centrifuges at nuclear facilities in Iran to spin so quickly that they tore themselves apart. Cyberwarfare has been identified by the Director of U.S. National Intelligence as the top threat to U.S. national security, in part due to incidents such as a data breach in which the records of nearly 14 million current and former U.S. government employees were stolen (Bremmer, 2015). In *The Hacker and the State,* Buchanan discusses the impact that cyberwarfare has had on geopolitics (Buchanan, 2020), which includes substantial damage and disruption to financial systems and critical infrastructure. The people and organisations behind such acts of cyberwarfare are often difficult to identify, or at least difficult for the government of the targeted country to publicly accuse within the constraints of international diplomacy. Nevertheless, there are some more well-known groups that are strongly suspected to be responsible for high-profile acts of cyberwarfare. The Lazarus Group for instance are a cybercrime organisation that became known in 2009. They are believed to operate primarily out of North Korea, although the exact status of the organisation and relationship with the North Korean government is not clear (White, 2022). They are alleged to be behind a large hack of Sony Pictures in 2014, an attack it has been suggested was prompted by a Sony Pictures movie called *The Interview,* which depicted a fictitious attempt to assassinate North Korean leader Kim Jong Un. The Lazarus Group have also been associated the WannaCry ransomware attack of 2017 that caused wide disruption to the health service in the UK, amongst other places, although as is often the case in cyber-attacks it is difficult to be completely sure who the instigators are. Similarly, a group known as Fancy Bear are believed to operate with the support of the Russian military intelligence agency GRU (Wintour, 2018). This group has been alleged to have been responsible for a range of cyber-attacks against Western organisations, including the Democratic National Committee in 2016, in what has been argued to have been an attempt to influence the outcome of the 2016 American presidential election. However, it is important to note that cyberwarfare acts are not limited to countries that are known for having adversarial relationships with the international community. The Computational Propaganda Project of 2017 conducted by scholars at the University of Oxford documented the behaviour of cyber troops in 28 countries, which included the United Kingdom, the United States, and several European countries (Bradshaw & Howard, 2018).

Atrews (2020) identifies some of the more well-known cyberwarfare attacks and suspected adversaries. This includes a cyberweapon known as Flame, believed to have originated from Israel and been designed to perform cyberespionage attacks throughout the Middle East. This malware included tools that allowed for remote screenshots of devices to be taken; microphones to be accessed; keylogging to be performed (recording of what keys the user has pressed); and erasing of data. Iran was the most heavily impacted of the countries who experienced this act of cyberwarfare. On the other hand, Disttrick, another form of malware, is believed to have been created in Iran. This is data wiping malware that targeted energy companies in the Middle East, causing extensive damage and disruption to the operation of companies including Saudi Aramco. Finally, DarkHotel is malware that targets specific guests at luxury hotels across Asia. The individuals targeted included Asian media executives, senior officials from government and non-government organisations, and U.S. executives. The primary targets appeared to be those located in North Korea, Japan, and India, with the attackers suspected to be based in South Korea. This example is notable for its use of social engineering techniques to target specific individuals.

As noted, although the targets of cyberwarfare are often considered in terms of nation states, these attacks can also focus on specific individuals as part of the overall strategy. For example, Atrews (2020) suggests that diplomats may be targeted at home by cyberespionage through devices including baby monitors, smartphones, computers, and their wi-fi network. Due to the sensitivities of international politics, there are few publicised cases of such cyberespionage, but there are incidents from cybersecurity that highlight the risks that can come from devices in the home. This is demonstrated by the case of computer tablets produced by the company VTech, the cameras and microphones of which were found to be accessible by hackers (Rhysider, 2017). This shows the ways in which technological devices are increasingly becoming weaponised, which reflects the Internet of Things (IoT). This refers to how devices are always interconnected to each other and to the internet or, in other words, it allows devices to be connected 'anytime, anyplace, with anything and anyone' (Friess et al., 2009). This creates further opportunities that cybercriminals can exploit – for instance a smart refrigerator that is connected to the internet for the purposes of notifying the user when a food item is running low may also be coopted by attackers into being part of a botnet.

Cyberwarfare can include influence operations, in which fake news, misinformation and disinformation are spread to a target country with the aim of influencing behaviour (Atrews, 2020). This relates to computational propaganda, which refers to the use of automation, algorithms and big data analytics to influence and deceive social media users (Woolley & Howard, 2016). The terms fake news, misinformation, and disinformation are often used interchangeably; however, a distinction is made between misinformation as an unintentional sharing of fake news (for example reposting false content on social media in the belief it is genuine), and disinformation as an intentional act of sharing fake news (American Psychiatric Association, 2023). In this text, 'fake news' is used broadly to refer to both acts of misinformation and disinformation, including social media manipulation when done with the goal of changing public opinion. Care should be taken however not to make assumptions about which countries engage in the propagation of fake news or, if they do, how this might be done. For example, Bolsover and Howard (2019) reported that, contrary to expectations, they found no evidence of bots posting pro-Chinese state content on Twitter. Instead, there was evidence of anti-China state viewpoints on Twitter, which appeared to be intended for Chinese diaspora and those within the country who had found ways to circumvent the block on using Twitter. The study also highlighted how the dissemination of fake news can vary between platforms, with there being little evidence of bots operating on Weibo, a Chinese microblogging site with some similarities to Twitter.

Acts of cyberwarfare are not limited to those aimed at other countries. Governments have been found to make use of private companies to spy on citizens, including through the use of malware (Frenkel, 2015). Governments and political parties also devote significant resources to utilise social media to influence opinion in both foreign and domestic populations (Bradshaw & Howard, 2017). Bradshaw and Howard (2018) refer to the state-sponsored organisations who disseminate fake news as cyber-troops. As they note, these organisations differ from individual hackers or hacktivist groups by being publicly funded and highly coordinated, with support from other government actors. It has been argued that authoritarian regimes have used social media and other internet technologies to exert further control and information management on their own citizens (Pearce & Kendzior, 2012). The use of fake news against other countries has also been observed, including notable examples such as the alleged involvement by the Russian government in the United Kingdom's referendum on leaving the European Union, and the 2016 United States election (Bradshaw & Howard, 2018). Whilst acts such as data theft and attempts to damage critical infrastructure have been referred to as 'hard power' capabilities the use of social media to influence behaviour and opinions has been described as 'soft power' (Bradshaw & Howard, 2018).

Theories of cybercrime

As Bossler (2017) observes, only a limited number of criminological studies relating to cybercrime have been published in the top criminology journals, something which Diamond and Bachmann (2015) have attributed to criminologists' lack of familiarity with the online cybercriminal ecosystem. Maimon and Louderback (2019) note that much of the research on cyber-dependent offenders is based on student or organisational samples, who primarily conduct low-level cybercrimes, and are not a representative sample of the many and varied different profiles of cybercriminals. The criminological theories that have been applied to cyber dependent crimes include the General Theory of Crime (Gottfredson & Hirschi, 1990), Social Learning Theory (Akers, 1973), Social Control Theory (Hirschi, 2017) and deterrence theories (Gibbs, 1968).

The General Theory of Crime distinguishes between criminality (the inclination or tendency to criminal behaviour) and crime (the actual act by which the law is broken). Gottfredson and Hirschi (1990) note that a crime can only take place when the propensity for crime coincides with an opportunity to commit a crime. Given the number of opportunities to commit crime that we typically encounter daily, it is the criminality of the individual that becomes the key factor. This is in turn linked to the level of self-control that the individual has. Gottfredson and Hirschi (1990) argue that this self-control is typically learned in early life. There is evidence to support this relationship between self-control and criminality amongst offline offenders (Pratt & Cullen, 2000), however research relating to online offenders is more mixed (Marcum, Higgins, Ricketts, & Wolfe, 2014). This proposed relationship is also part of Social Control Theory (Hirschi, 2017), which has been described as one of the turning points in the history of criminology (Costello & Laub, 2020). In contrast to criminological theories that focus on motivations for delinquency, Social Control Theory instead focuses on the restraints and circumstances that prevent delinquency. The theory states that criminality comes from an individual having a lack of intimate attachments, aspirations, and moral beliefs that bind people to mainstream, legitimate lifestyles. This is an interesting point to consider in relation to cybercrime. As will again be discussed in Chapter 3, individuals who become involved in cybercrime often do so as part of a group. Trust relationships form between the members of cybercriminal groups, even if they do not know each other's real-world identity. Hacking forums appear to be important sources of self-esteem, self-identity, and social relationships to forum members, and analyses of hacking forums, albeit surface web ones, suggest that members are concerned with questions of morality (McAlaney, Hambidge, Kimpton, & Thackray, 2020).

Social leaning theory in relation to crime (Akers, 1973) refers to how criminal behaviour is learned through social processes. This is related to Bandura's (1977) social learning theory, but with a focus on operant conditioning as the driver of criminal behaviour. Operant conditioning, also known as instrumental conditioning, states that behaviour that is positively reinforced with some type of reward is likely to be repeated, whereas behaviour that is punished will be less likely to be repeated. Negative reinforcement can also occur, where the frequency of a behaviour is increased through the removal of a negative stimulus (Skinner, 1963). For example, if a child refuses to eat a certain food at mealtimes, and the parent acquiesces and removes that food item, then negative reinforcement may occur where the child is more likely to refuse that food in future. As such, Akers (1973) suggests that whether individuals become involved in crime in the long term depends on their initial experiences of criminal activities, as well as their interactions with others who are engaged in criminal activities. If they are punished because of these actions then their future involvement in criminal activity becomes less likely, but if they are rewarded then their future involvement in criminal activity becomes more likely. It is possible to envisage how these processes may operate in relation to cyberspace. As noted, there is a lack of understanding and public awareness of many forms of cybercrime, something that may also be applied to some elements of law enforcement (Halder, 2022). Legislation pertaining to cybercrime is often outdated, and not fit for purpose (Mishra, 2022 #9918). As such the people who get involved in cybercriminal activities may be able to do so without being detected or may not face adequate punishment if they are caught. As will be discussed further in Chapter 3, such individuals may also be rewarded through the social support and approval they can receive through becoming part of hacking communities. They may also come to these hacking communities through engagement in other communities. In support of this, Hutchings and Clayton (2016) have identified that participation in online gaming communities can result in participation in hacking. Similarly, it has been found that spending time in chatrooms and on social media may mean that they are presented with more reinforcement of online deviance, as well as being provided with a social norm of deviance (Donner, 2016; Weulen Kranenbarg, Holt, & van Gelder, 2019).

Deterrence theory assumes that people make reasoned decisions towards committing or abstaining from crime based on the maximisation of their benefits and minimisation of their costs (Beccaria, 1963). As observed by D'Arcy & Herath (2011), classic deterrence theory focuses on formal (legal) sanctions and argues that the swifter and more severe the sanctions, the more individuals are deterred from engaging in the relevant behaviour (Gibbs, 1975). Revisions to the original theory include informal sanctions such as social disapproval, self-disapproval (i.e., feelings of shame), and moral inhibition (Piquero & Tibbetts, 1996). More recently, deterrence theory has included perceived risks and costs of both informal and formal sanctions as part of the decision-making process an individual uses when considering whether to engage in criminal activity (Pratt, Cullen, Blevins, Daigle, & Madensen, 2006). This theory has been applied within cybersecurity, with D'Arcy & Herath (2011) commenting that it is one of the more widely used theories in the field. Nevertheless, they also note that the evidence base for the application of deterrence theory to cybersecurity contains mixed results, in part due to methodological inconsistences in how sanctions have been conceptualised and measured.

Routine activity theory (Cohen & Felson, 1979) has been discussed in relation to cybercrime (An & Kim, 2018). This theory states that crime is likely to occur when there are three elements present: a motivated offender, an attractive target, and an absence of capable guardianship. As will be discussed in greater detail in Chapter 3, there are many and varied motivations for individuals to engage in cybercriminal acts. There is also a surfeit of attractive targets, which within the context of routine activities theory refers to a target that the attacker perceives to be vulnerable and from whom something can – relatively speaking – be easily obtained. The lack of capable guardianship in the offline context could mean for instance the lack of security guards in a store to deter shoplifting. Online, this could be applied to many activities. For example, the IT staff within an organisation could be guardians of the workplace IT systems. Similarly, the use of firewalls and up to date software could be considered as a form of technological guardianship. In both cases though this guardianship is only effective if the human undertakes certain required actions to engage with those guardians, or indeed not seek to circumvent restrictions imposed by guardians, such as bypassing software updates. These tensions between whose responsibility it is to ensure protection from cybercrime reflect the larger perception of humans as being the weak link of cybersecurity. This is discussed in greater detail in Chapter 4.

Protection Motivation Theory (Rogers, 1975) has also been applied to cybersecurity behaviours (Hassandoust & Techatassanasoontorn, 2020). This theory relates to how people respond when they feel threatened, as based on two elements – how likely they think they are to be exposed to that threat, and how severe that threat could be if it occurred. Based on these factors, the individual decides whether they need to take action to avoid this threat. For example, we may recognise that it is a common experience to catch the flu, but many people will perceive this as having a low severity, as in being unlikely to cause us serious harm. A plane crash on the other hand is something that potentially has a very severe outcome but is something that an individual is extremely unlikely to experience. Of course, individual characteristics and beliefs are relevant to these processes. Whilst most people may not perceive the flu to be a threat there are individuals who are immunocompromised or who have other health issues from whom any respiratory infection can be a serious threat. It is likely that perceptions of the severity of respiratory illness also changed during the COVID-19 pandemic, highlighting how temporal changes in the broader social environment can influence perceptions of likelihood and threat. Similarly, an individual with a fear of flying may objectively accept that flying is one of the safest forms of travel, but they still subjectively and emotionally feel threatened by the experience of flying. The use of Protection Motivation Theory in cyber-security behaviours is discussed in more detail in Chapter 6.

Overall, these theories share some commonalities such as the social environment, self-control, the perception of risk, and self-identity. There is no single theory that could be said to be universally accepted and applied to understanding cybercriminal behaviour, although neither is there any such theory that is solely used to explain offline criminal behaviour. Nevertheless, these theories provide useful insights into how to predict, identify, and predict cybercrime, although there remains a need for further research into the psychological aspects of cybercrime. This includes a better understanding of how cybercrime can differ from offline crime. This is something that is likely to always be a moving target, as technologies continue to evolve and develop in ways that cannot be predicted.

References

Abramson, L. Y., Seligman, M. E. P., & Teasdale, J. D. (1978). Learned helplessness in humans: critique and reformulation. *Journal of Abnormal Psychology, 87*(1), 49–74. doi:10.1037/0021-843x.87.1.49

Agatston, P., & Limber, S. (2018). Cyberbullying prevention and intervention: Promising approaches and recommendations for further evaluation. In U'Mofe Gordon, J. (ed.), *Bullying prevention and intervention at school: Integrating theory and research into best practices* (pp. 73–93). Cham, Switzerland: Springer Nature.

Akers, R. L. (1973). *Deviant behavior: A social learning approach*. Belmont, CA: Wadsworth.

American Psychiatric Association. (2023). Misinformation and disinformation. Retrieved from https://www.apa.org/topics/journalism-facts/misinformation-disinformation

An, J., & Kim, H.-W. (2018). A Data Analytics Approach to the Cybercrime Underground Economy. *IEEE Access, 6*. doi:10.1109/ACCESS.2018.2831667

Atrews, R. A. (2020). Cyberwarfare Threats, Security, Attacks, and Impact. *Journal of Information Warfare, 19*(4), 17–28. Retrieved from https://www-jstor-org.bournemouth.idm.oclc.org/stable/27033642

Bandura, A. (1977). *Social learning theory*. Englewood Cliffs, N.J.: Prentice Hall.

Bartlett, J. (2014). *The Dark Net: Inside the Digital Underworld.* London: William Heinemann.

Bartlett, J. (2022). *The missing cryptoqueen: the billion dollar cryptocurrency con and the woman who got away with it* (First US edition). New York: Hatchette Books.

BBC News. (2016). Total Wipeout: The non-existent tour which thousands signed up for. Retrieved from https://www.bbc.co.uk/news/uk-england-35744044

BBC News. (2017). NHS cyber-attack: GPs and hospitals hit by ransomware. *BBC News.* Retrieved from https://www.bbc.co.uk/news/health-39899646

Beccaria, C. (1963). *On Crimes and Punishment.* New York: Macmillan.

Bolsover, G., & Howard, P. (2019). Chinese computational propaganda: automation, algorithms and the manipulation of information about Chinese politics on Twitter and Weibo. *Information Communication & Society, 22*(14), 2063–2080. doi:10.1080/1369118x.2018.1476576

Bossler, A. M. (2017). Need for Debate on the Implications of Honeypot Data for Restrictive Deterrence Policies in Cyberspace. *Criminology & Public Policy, 16*(3), 681–688. doi:https://doi.org/10.1111/1745-9133.12322

Bradshaw, S., & Howard, P. N. (2017). *Troops, Trolls and Troublemakers: A Global Inventory of Organized Social Media Manipulation.* Retrieved from http://comprop.oii.ox.ac.uk/wp-content/uploads/sites/89/2017/07/Troops-Trolls-and-Troublemakers.pdf

Bradshaw, S., & Howard, P. N. (2018). THE GLOBAL ORGANIZATION OF SOCIAL MEDIA DISINFORMATION CAMPAIGNS. *Journal of International Affairs, 71*(1.5), 23–32. Retrieved from https://www.jstor.org/stable/26508115

Brandwatch. (2019). 53 Incredible Facebook Statistics and Facts. Retrieved from https://www.brandwatch.com/blog/facebook-statistics/

Bremmer, I. (2015). These 5 facts explain the threat of cyber warfare. *Time.* Retrieved from https://time.com/3928086/these-5-facts-explain-the-threat-of-cyber-warfare/

Brenner, S. (2003). Organized Cybercrime? How Cyberspace May Affect the Structure of Criminal Relationships. *N.C. J.L. & Tech.* 4 (1).

Brewer, R., Fox, S., & Miller, C. (2019). Applying the Techniques of Neutralization to the Study of Cybercrime. In Holt, T., Bossler, A. (Eds), *The Palgrave Handbook of International Cybercrime and Cyberdeviance* (pp. 1–19). Cham, Switzerland: Palgrave Macmillan.

Buchanan, B. (2020). *The hacker and the state: cyber attacks and the new normal of geopolitics.* Cambridge, MA: Harvard University Press.

Casciani, D. (2017). Briton who knocked Liberia offline with cyber attack jailed. Retrieved from https://www.bbc.co.uk/news/uk-46840461

Chen, H. Chiang, R. H. L. & Storey, V. C. (2012). Business Intelligence and Analytics: From Big Data to Big Impact. *MIS Quarterly, 36*(4), 1165. doi:10.2307/41703503

Choo, K.-K. R., & Smith, R. (2008). Criminal exploitation of online systems by organised crime groups. *Asian Journal of Criminology, 3*, 37–59. doi:10.1007/s11417-007-9035-y

Cohen, L. E., & Felson, M. (1979). Social Change and Crime Rate Trends: A Routine Activity Approach. *American Sociological Review, 44*(4), 588–608. doi:10.2307/2094589

Coleman, G. (2014). *Hacker, Hoaxer, Whistleblower, Spy: The Many Faces Of Anonymous.* London: Verso.

Connolly, L., & Doble, A. (2017). Is your postman delivering drugs? Retrieved from https://www.bbc.co.uk/news/newsbeat-38223838

Costello, B. J., & Laub, J. H. (2020). Social Control Theory: The Legacy of Travis Hirschi's Causes of Delinquency. *Annual Review of Criminology, 3*(1), 21–41. doi:10.1146/annurev-criminol-011419-041527

Crown Prosecution Service. (2023). Cybercrime - prosecution guidance. Retrieved from https://www.cps.gov.uk/legal-guidance/cybercrime-prosecution-guidance

CybSafe. (2022). *Oh, Behave! The Annual Cybersecurity Attitudes and Behaviors Report 2022.* Retrieved from https://www.cybsafe.com/whitepapers/cybersecurity-attitudes-and-behaviors-report/

D'Arcy, J., & Herath, T. (2011). A review and analysis of deterrence theory in the IS security literature: making sense of the disparate findings. *European Journal of Information Systems, 20*(6), 643–658. doi:10.1057/ejis.2011.23

Décary-Hétu, D., & Dupont, B. (2012). The social network of hackers. *Global Crime, 13*(3), 160–175. doi:10.1080/17440572.2012.702523

DEF CON. (2023). Archives. Retrieved from https://defcon.org/html/links/dc-archives.html

Department of Culture Media and Sport. (2022). *Cyber Security Breaches Survey 2022.* Retrieved from https://www.gov.uk/government/statistics/cyber-security-breaches-survey-2022/cyber-security-breaches-survey-2022

Diamond, B., & Bachmann, M. (2015). Out of the Beta Phase: Obstacles, Challenges, and Promising Paths in the Study of Cyber Criminology. *International Journal of Cyber Criminology, 9*, 24–34.

Donner, C. (2016). The Gender Gap and Cybercrime: An Examination of College Students' Online Offending. *Victims & Offenders, 11*, 1–22. doi:10.1080/15564886.2016.1173157

Frenkel, S. (2015). These two companies are helping governments spy on their citizens. Retrieved from https://www.buzzfeednews.com/article/sheerafrenkel/meet-the-companies-whose-business-is-letting-governments-spy#.tvM9gEPmEV

Friess, P., Guillemin, P., Gusmeroli, S., Sundmaeker, H., Bassi, A., Jubert, I., & Doody, P. (2009). Internet of things strategic research roadmap. *The Cluster of European Research Projects.*

Furnell, S., Emm, D., & Papadaki, M. (2015). The challenge of measuring cyber-dependent crimes. *Computer Fraud & Security, 2015*(10), 5–12. doi:https://doi.org/10.1016/S1361-3723(15)30093-2

Gibbs, J. P. (1968). Crime, punishment, and deterrence. *The Southwestern Social Science Quarterly, 48*(4), 515–530.

Gibbs, J. P. (1975). *Crime, punishment, and deterrence.* New York: Elsevier.

Goldsmith, A., & Brewer, R. (2015). Digital drift and the criminal interaction order. *Theoretical Criminology, 19*(1), 112–130. doi:10.1177/1362480614538645

Gottfredson, M. R., & Hirschi, T. (1990). *A general theory of crime.* Redwood City, CA: Stanford University Press.

Grabosky, P. (2016). The evolution of cybercrime, 2006–2016. In Holt, T. J. (Ed.), *Cybercrime Through an Interdisciplinary Lens.* New York: Routledge.

Greenberg, A. (2022). *Tracers in the dark: the global hunt for the crime lords of cryptocurrency* (First edition). New York: Doubleday.

Halder, D. (2022). *Cyber victimology: decoding cyber crime victimization.* New York: Routledge.

Hassandoust, F., & Techatassanasoontorn, A. A. (2020). Understanding users' information security awareness and intentions: A full nomology of protection motivation theory. In Benson, V. & McAlaney, J. (Eds), *Cyber Influence and Cognitive Threats* (pp. 129–143). London: Academic Press. A previous version of this paper was published in the Proceedings of the 22nd Pacific Asia Conference on Information Systems, 26–30 June 2018, Yokohama, Japan.

Hirschi, T. (2017). *Causes of delinquency.* London: Routledge.

Holroyd, M. (2022). Gridlock as hackers order hundreds of taxis to same place in Moscow. Retrieved from https://www.euronews.com/my-europe/2022/09/02/gridlock-as-hackers-order-hundreds-of-taxis-to-same-place-in-moscow

Holt, T. J. (2007). Subcultural evolution? Examining the influence of on- and off-line experiences on deviant subcultures. *Deviant Behavior, 28*(2), 171–198. doi:10.1080/01639620601131065

Holt, T. J., Bossler, A. M., & May, D. C. (2012). Low Self-Control, Deviant Peer Associations, and Juvenile Cyberdeviance. *American Journal of Criminal Justice, 37*(3), 378–395. doi:10.1007/s12103-011-9117-3

Huang, C., Guo, Y., Guo, W., & Li, Y. (2021). HackerRank: Identifying key hackers in underground forums. *International Journal of Distributed Sensor Networks, 17*(5), 15501477211015145. doi:10.1177/15501477211015145

Hutchings, A., & Clayton, R. (2016). Exploring the Provision of Online Booter Services. *Deviant Behavior, 37*(10), 1163–1178. doi:10.1080/01639625.2016.1169829

Hutson, E., Kelly, S., & Militello, L. K. (2018). Systematic Review of Cyberbullying Interventions for Youth and Parents With Implications for Evidence-Based Practice. *Worldviews Evid Based Nurs, 15*(1), 72–79. doi:10.1111/wvn.12257

Iuga, C., Nurse, J. R. C., & Erola, A. (2016). Baiting the hook: factors impacting susceptibility to phishing attacks. *Human-centric Computing and Information Sciences, 6*(1), 8. doi:10.1186/s13673-016-0065-2

Kabasinskas, A., & Sutiene, K. (2021). Key Roles of Crypto-Exchanges in Generating Arbitrage Opportunities. *Entropy, 23*(4). doi:10.3390/e23040455

Kearney, W. D., & Kruger, H. A. (2016). Can perceptual differences account for enigmatic information security behaviour in an organisation? *Computers & Security, 61*, 46–58. doi:http://dx.doi.org/10.1016/j.cose.2016.05.006

Kelion, L. (2016). Nissan Leaf electric cars hack vulnerability disclosed. Retrieved from https://www.bbc.co.uk/news/technology-35642749

Kerner, S. M. (2022). Colonial Pipeline hack explained: Everything you need to know. Retrieved from https://www.techtarget.com/whatis/feature/Colonial-Pipeline-hack-explained-Everything-you-need-to-know

Khandelwal, S. (2016). Europol arrests 34 teenagers for using DDoS attack tools. Retrieved from https://thehackernews.com/2016/12/ddos-attack-tool.html

Kraemer-Mbula, E., Tang, P., & Rush, H. (2013). The cybercrime ecosystem: Online innovation in the shadows? *Technological Forecasting and Social Change, 80*(3), 541–555. doi:https://doi.org/10.1016/j.techfore.2012.07.002

Kremling, J., & Parker, A. M. (2017). *Cyberspace, Cybersecurity and Cybercrime.* Thousand Oaks, CA: SAGE.

Lawrence, D. (2014). The inside story of Tor, the best internet anonymity tool the Government ever built. *Bloomberg Businessweek.* Retrieved from https://www.bloomberg.com/news/articles/2014-01-23/tor-anonymity-software-vs-dot-the-national-security-agency?leadSource=uverify%20wall

Lee, D. (2016). Instagram hacked by 10-year-old boy. Retrieved from https://www.bbc.co.uk/news/technology-36200012

Lewis, J. A. (2018). Economic impact of cybercrime—At $600 billion and counting–No slowing down. *Center for Strategic and International Studies Report (21/2/2018).* Retrieved from https://www.csis.org/analysis/economic-impact-cybercrime

Lima, A. Q., & Keegan, B. (2020). Challenges of using machine learning algorithms for cybersecurity: a study of threat-classification models applied to social media communication data. In Benson, V. & McAlaney, J. (Eds), *Cyber Influence and Cognitive Threats* (pp. 33–52). London: Academic Press.

Macdonald, M., & Frank, R. (2017). The network structure of malware development, deployment and distribution. *Global Crime, 18*(1), 49–69. doi:10.1080/17440572.2016.1227707

Maimon, D., & Louderback, E. R. (2019). Cyber-dependent crimes: An interdisciplinary review. *Annual Review of Criminology, 2*(1), 191–216. doi:10.1146/annurev-criminol-032317-092057

Marcum, C. D., Higgins, G. E., Ricketts, M. L., & Wolfe, S. E. (2014). Hacking in High School: Cybercrime Perpetration by Juveniles. *Deviant Behavior, 35*(7), 581–591. doi:10.1080/01639625.2013.867721

Marshall, A., & Stephens, P. (2008). Identity and identity theft. In Bryant, R. (Ed.), *Investigating Digital Crime* (pp. 179–193). Chichester: John Wiley & Sons.

McAlaney, J., Hambidge, S., Kimpton, E., & Thackray, H. (2020). *Knowledge is power: An analysis of discussions on hacking forums.* Paper presented at the 2020 IEEE European Symposium on Security and Privacy Workshops (EuroS&PW).

McGuire, M. (2012). *Organised crime in the digital age.* London: John Grieve Centre for Policing and Security.

Morris, S. (2021). Plymouth shooter fascinated by serial killers and 'incel' culture, inquest hears. *The Guardian.* Retrieved from https://www.theguardian.com/uk-news/2023/jan/18/plymouth-shooter-jake-davison-fascinated-by-mass-shootings-and-incel-culture-inquest-hears

Nee, C., & Meenaghan, A. K. (2020). Using simulated environments to understand offender decision making. In Burrell, A. & Tonkin, M. (Eds), *Property Crime: Criminological and Psychological Perspectives.* London: Routledge.

Newman, L. H. (2023). Whar Twitter's 200 Million-User Email Leak Actually Means. Retrieved from https://www.wired.com/story/twitter-leak-200-million-user-email-addresses/

Nurse, J. (2015). Exploring the Risks to Identity Security and Privacy in Cyberspace. *XRDS: Crossroads, The ACM Magazine for Students, 21*, 42–47. doi:10.1145/2730912

Olson, P. (2012). *We Are Anonymous.* New York: Back Bay Books.

Ostrom, E. (1998). A behavioral approach to the rational choice theory of collective action. *American Political Science Review, 92*(1), 1–22. doi:10.2307/2585925

Pearce, K. E., & Kendzior, S. (2012). Networked Authoritarianism and Social Media in Azerbaijan. *Journal of Communication, 62*, 283–298.

Piquero, A., & Tibbetts, S. (1996). Specifying the direct and indirect effects of low self-control and situational factors in offenders' decision making: Toward a more complete model of rational offending. *Justice Quarterly, 13*(3), 481–510. doi:10.1080/07418829600093061

Pratt, T., & Cullen, F. (2000). The empirical status of Gottfredson and Hirschi's general theory of crime: A meta-analysis. *Criminology, 38*, 931–964. doi:10.1111/j.1745-9125.2000.tb00911.x

Pratt, T., Cullen, F. T., Blevins, K., Daigle, L., & Madensen, T. D. (2006). The Empirical Status of Deterrence Theory: A Meta-Analysis. *TAKING STOCK, 15*, 367–395.

Reynolds, K. (2023). Editorial: It Sure Looks Like the U.S. Is Trying to Kill Crypto. Retrieved from https://www.coindesk.com/consensus-magazine/2023/03/30/coindesk-editorial-it-sure-looks-like-the-us-is-trying-to-kill-crypto/

Rhysider, J. (2017). *Episode 2: The Peculiar Case of the VTech Hacker.* Retrieved from https://darknetdiaries.com/episode/2/

Rogers, R. W. (1975). A protection motivation theory of fear appeals and attitude change. *Journal of Psychology, 91*(1), 93–114.

Skinner, B. F. (1963). Operant behavior. *American Psychologist, 18*(8), 503–515. doi:10.1037/h0045185

Sood, A. K., & Enbody, R. J. (2013). Crimeware-as-a-service—A survey of commoditized crimeware in the underground market. *International Journal of Critical Infrastructure Protection, 6*(1), 28–38. doi:https://doi.org/10.1016/j.ijcip.2013.01.002

Steinmetz, K. F. (2014). Craft(y)ness: An Ethnographic Study of Hacking. *The British Journal of Criminology, 55*(1), 125–145. doi:10.1093/bjc/azu061

Sugiura, L. (2021). *The incel rebellion: the rise of the manosphere and the virtual war against women* (First edition). Bingley, UK: Emerald Publishing Limited.

Suler, J. (2004). The online disinhibition effect. *Cyberpsychology & Behaviour, 7*(3), 321–326. doi:10.1089/1094931041291295

Tam, L., Glassman, M., & Vandenwauver, M. (2010). The psychology of password management: a tradeoff between security and convenience. *Behaviour & Information Technology, 29*(3), 233–244. doi:Doi 10.1080/01449290903121386

Tseloni, A., Mailley, J., Farrell, G., & Tilley, N. (2010). Exploring the international decline in crime rates. *European Journal of Criminology, 7*(5), 375–394. doi:10.1177/1477370810367014

Vaillancourt, T., Faris, R., & Mishna, F. (2017). Cyberbullying in Children and Youth: Implications for Health and Clinical Practice. *The Canadian Journal of Psychiatry, 62*(6), 368–373. doi:10.1177/0706743716684791

Walls, D. S. (2001). *Crime and the Internet.* New York: Routledge.

Weulen Kranenbarg, M., Holt, T. J., & van Gelder, J.-L. (2019). Offending and Victimization in the Digital Age: Comparing Correlates of Cybercrime and Traditional Offending-Only, Victimization-Only and the Victimization-Offending Overlap. *Deviant Behavior, 40*(1), 40–55. doi:10.1080/01639625.2017.1411030

White, G. (2022). *The Lazarus Heist: From Hollywood to High Finance: Inside North Korea's Global Cyber War.* London: Penguin.

Wilcox, P. (2018, 5/12/2018). Drawing the line for cyber warfare. *Computer Weekly.* Retrieved from tinyurl.com/bdhar7mh

Wintour, P. (2018). UK accuses Kremlin of ordering series of 'reckless' cyber-attacks. Retrieved from https://www.theguardian.com/technology/2018/oct/04/uk-accuses-kremlin-of-ordering-series-of-reckless-cyber-attacks

Woolley, S. C., & Howard, P. N. (2016). Automation, Algorithms, and Politics | Political Communication, Computational Propaganda, and Autonomous Agents — Introduction. *International Journal of Communication; Vol 10 (2016).* Retrieved from https://ijoc.org/index.php/ijoc/article/view/6298

Zhu, C. Y., Huang, S. Q., Evans, R., & Zhang, W. (2021). Cyberbullying Among Adolescents and Children: A Comprehensive Review of the Global Situation, Risk Factors, and Preventive Measures. *Frontiers in Public Health, 9.* doi:10.3389/fpubh.2021.634909

Social engineering 2

Context

Social engineering within the context of cybersecurity refers to the use of psychological manipulation to influence the target into conducting an action that contributes to the breach of a system. An example of this that many will be familiar with are phishing emails, which make use of a range of psychological manipulations to encourage the target to click on a link or to open an attachment, such as the use of urgency, emotional appeals, or authority. Examples of this would be emails that claim to be from a tax authority, stating that the recipient is in breach of some tax law and will face punitive measures if they do not urgently act. This will typically involve the target being asked to click on a link or open an attachment, both of which will contain malicious software that will infect the device and system the person is using. One reason why phishing emails are so popular as a social engineering technique is that they require little effort or cost to the attacker, and only require engagement by one person in the target population to potentially be successful. In other words, it does not matter if a target organisation has 10 employees or 100,000 employees – only one employee must click on the malicious link or file for the attackers to potentially access the system. Technological approaches such as firewalls and anti-virus software can block some of the risks posed by phishing emails, but not all of them. In addition, phishing emails are one example of social engineering, but other types of attack exist, as will be discussed in this chapter.

Social engineering has been argued to be the single biggest threat in cybersecurity (Salahdine & Kaabouch, 2019). Social engineering is not limited to cybercrime. For example in 2016, employees in several fast food restaurants in

DOI: 10.4324/9781003300359-2

the USA were targeted and tricked into smashing the restaurant windows on the basis of them believing there was a gas leak within the building (Almasy, 2016). There is limited published academic research on social engineering, and very little about the life experiences and characteristics of social engineers. There are however some books written by high profile social engineers which discuss their perspectives on social engineering and the experiences they have had that led them into social engineering. One of the more well-known examples of this is *Social Engineering: The Art of Human Hacking*, authored by the high-profile social engineer Chris Hadnagy in 2011. A revised version of this book was published in 2018, entitled *Social Engineering: The Science of Human Hacking* (Hadnagy, 2018). This change in 'Art' to 'Science' was, as Hadnagy explains in the more recent text, a recognition of the growing research evidence on the psychological processes that underpin social engineering techniques. Nevertheless, there remains a surprising lack of application of the research literature to real world examples of social engineering techniques.

Hadnagy (2018) and other social engineers provides services in which they test how resilient an organisation is to a social engineering attack. This is a form of penetration testing, which is a common activity in cybersecurity (Al-Ahmad, Kahtan, Hujainah, & Jalab, 2019). It involves a post deployment vulnerability assessment task that is conducted as an isolated test process in a manual and sometimes ad hoc manner (Zhao, Shang, Wan, & Zeng, 2015), or 'as the art of finding an open door' (Geer & Harthorne, 2002). It could be argued that the phrase 'penetration testing' is still often assumed to refer solely to technological means of testing defences (e.g., through what might traditionally considered to be hacking) rather than through social engineering. Hadnagy (2018) notes however that there is increasing awareness of social engineering, both as a threat from malicious actors and as an important component of a comprehensive penetration test. This is in part due to increased media attention, and to the interesting experiences and stories described by social engineers (Radcliffe, 2023). In the case of Hadnagy and Radcliffe, the service they and other similar professionals offer is referred to as ethical social engineering, in which they apply the technique used by criminal social engineers to help organisations understand how to better protect themselves.

Social engineering techniques

Hadnagy (2018) argues that a social engineering attack is composed of the following steps:

- OSINT (Open-Source Intelligence)
- Pretext development

- Attack plan
- Attack launch
- Reporting

OSINT, or open-source intelligence, refers to the information that the social engineer collects about the target or other relevant actors to be able to conduct the attack. As the name suggests, this intelligence gathering is typically done through open sources which are readily available in the public domain. This can include simply searching for the target online, to find out for example their interests and hobbies. The increasing availability of this type of information through social media platforms is something that social engineers have acknowledged as being enormously useful in their activities (Radcliffe, 2023). Alternatively, OSINT could include looking at the management structure displayed on a company website, to ascertain which individuals should be targeted. This could be anyone at any level of the company from the CEO to lower paid employees, depending on the plan that the social engineer has in mind. Cleaning staff for example may, on the surface, have little power within an organisation, but they typically have access to every office within a company. The social engineer may also visit the physical premises of a company that is to be targeted, to observe for example what type of clothing employees wear, where the entry and exit doors are, whether there are security requirements for entry, and how the lobby is set up. Depending on the nature of the business it may also be possible to enter the premises and walk around. Social engineers comment how easily this can often be done, particularly if they equip themselves with some props and appropriate clothing such as a clipboard or high visibility jacket (Radcliffe, 2023; Rhysider, 2023). As discussed in more detail later in this chapter, this reflects the cognitive biases that humans use to navigate their social world and leads people to come to erroneous conclusions about whether the social engineer they have seen has a legitimate right to be in that building.

This OSINT contributes towards the development of the pretext, which is the backstory that the individual presents themselves with. An example given by Hadnagy (2011) is that of a social engineer who was employed by a well-known theme park. After using OSINT to determine some basic aspects of the setup of the theme park and the software they used, the social engineer arrived at the ticket desk with his family in attendance. By presenting a pretext of being on holiday and having experienced issues with printing out their tickets, the social engineer was able to persuade the person behind the ticket desk to open a PDF file from his email account, using the PC at the ticket desk. This PDF contained the malicious software that was needed to demonstrate to the theme park their systems could have been breached, although as this was a case of penetration testing so no actual harm was done. An interesting point of this case study was that the social engineer was able to determine what version of the PDF software the theme park was currently using by phoning them directly and pretending to be salesman who was selling an alternative software. The theme park employee who spoke to the social engineer presumably freely provided this information because the question did not seem to be sensitive. This is a common theme in social engineering attacks – each individual step or interaction with the target does not, by itself, appear to be posing a threat. It is only when the information gathered is put together that the true risk is apparent.

The plan for attacks such as the one above is broken down into what, when, and who. This is of interest as aligns to the common policing investigation technique of considering the 5WH of an offence – what, when, where, who, why and how (College of Policing, 2013). In relation to penetration testing, 'what' refers to what will happen in the attack, and what the goals are. Radcliffe (2023) observes that there can be some tensions when setting goals with an organisation when a social engineering penetration test is being planned. The organisation may feel that some assets are too sensitive to be exposed to someone external to that organisation, even if that person is being brought in as a security advisor. Similarly, there may be debates around how many people within the organisation will be informed in advance that a penetration test is going to occur. To be a true test of the security of an organisation as few people as possible should be aware that the test is occurring, but organisations may not feel comfortable with some individuals, such as members of senior management, not having advanced knowledge (Radcliffe, 2023). Finally, organisations are unlikely of course to want the social engineer to steal any sensitive products or data. As such an alternative must be agreed upon, such as the social engineering taking photographs from within a secure location, leaving behind a calling card, or sending an email from a device inside the organisation (Radcliffe, 2023). Once the tests are set, the next step is to decide upon when to launch the attack. This is linked to the 'who' in the attack plan, which refers to who needs to be available to implement or assist with the plan – although often without realising that their actions are in fact facilitating an attack. The plan is then set and the attack is launched, although social engineers note that an overly detailed plan can act as an impediment if something unexpected happens (Hadnagy, 2018; Radcliffe, 2023). In ethical social engineering the final stage then is to report the findings of the attack to the client, with advice on how to change their practices to reduce the risk of becoming the victim of a criminal social engineering attack. A recurring theme from accounts given by ethical social engineers and penetration testers is how overconfident organisations often are that their systems are secure; and in turn how shocked they are with the ease with which they have been breached (Hadnagy, 2018; Radcliffe, 2023; Rhysider, 2023).

The trickery used by social engineers and hackers does not need to be complicated to be successful. For example, it has been reported that hackers send USB sticks infected with malware to U.S. companies disguised as gifts (Ropek, 2022). As with phishing emails, it does not matter if most of these USB sticks are not never plugged in – it only requires one employee to insert the USB stick into a company device for the attack to potentially be successful. The ease with which people can be manipulated into facilitating cyber-attacks can be surprising. In one study, psychology students approached passers-by and asked them if they would participate in a short survey on IT behaviour, being conducted by the local university (Happ, Melzer, & Steffgen, 2016). As part of this, participants were asked to tell the interviewer what their password was to their computer or device. Participants were also offered a chocolate, either at the start of the interview, directly before being asked for their password, or at the end of the interview. One third of participants provided their password on request. Of those who did not 70% still provided some form of hint of their password. 48% of those who were given the chocolate immediately before being asked for their password provided it, in contrast to those given the chocolate at the start of the interview (40%) or not given a chocolate at all (30%). However, the effect of being given a chocolate was only significant for male participants. Female participants were not influenced by this. In addition, older participants were less likely to reveal their password. It should be noted however that research into who is most likely to be a victim of cybercrime has produced conflicting results, as is expanded on in Chapter 4.

Social engineering exploits heuristics and cognitive biases. These are the mental shortcuts that we use as humans to cope with the vast amount of information that we must process daily to be able to navigate our social worlds. For instance, we will typically assume that anyone wearing the uniform or clothing of an organisation is a part of that organisation, such as if someone wearing the overalls associated with a cleaning company is an employee of that company. Most of the time this would be a reasonable assumption to make, and it would be impractical for employees in a company to ask everyone wearing a cleaner's uniform to provide proof that they are a legitimate employee of that cleaning company. This is of course something that is exploited by social engineers, who may for instance gain access to an organisation simply by purchasing some similar uniforms and walking, unchallenged, around an organisation. Similarly, phishing emails will often include a logo that matches the organisation that the phishing email is purporting to be from, such as the logo of a bank. In both cases the attacker is exploiting the fact that individuals will come to quick conclusions about the legitimacy of what they are seeing, due to these visual cues.

There have been many specific types of heuristics and cognitive biases identified in the psychological literature (Hasenstab, 2013), many of which in turn could feasibly be exploited by social engineers and attackers. These include biases and heuristics that influence emotions, memory, and perceptions of risk and probability. Due to the lack of psychological research on social engineering however there are fewer studies than could be expected that explicitly identify specific heuristic and cognitive biases in cases of social engineering. Nevertheless, some relevant studies have been conducted. For instance, Iuga, Nurse, and Erola (2016) found evidence for the anchoring effect in their study of phishing websites. The anchoring effect is a cognitive bias identified by Northcraft and Neale (1987), in which individuals over-rely on the first piece of information they are presented with. Northcraft and Neale's study for example found that presenting people with an erroneous estimation of the value of a property influenced that person's valuation of the property. This occurred even when the individual concerned was a real estate agent, i.e., an expert who it could be expected would come to an objective and rational conclusion. In the study by Iuga et al. (2016) a similar phenomenon was observed, in which participants' views of the legitimacy of a phishing website was influenced by their initial judgement of that website.

There are some challenges around the terminology used to describe heuristics and cognitive biases, which is a representation of the wider views in cybersecurity of the challenges inherent in predicting human behaviour. It could be argued that the term 'heuristic' is more often used in an objective manner to refer to any mental shortcut that an individual uses. On the other hand, 'cognitive bias' tends to have more negative connotations, and suggests that the use of heuristic has led to an unwanted outcome. In the case of the latter, the implication is that cognitive biases are a flaw of human cognition, and one which makes it difficult for cybersecurity practitioners to ensure that socio-technical systems are safe. Simply put, the existence of cognitive biases can lead to the view that humans are inherently unpredictable, unreliable, and irrational, and a source of irritation to cybersecurity practitioners who despair at the inability of humans to behave sensibly when using computer systems. However, the counterview from psychological research would be that these heuristics and cognitive purposes are not a flaw in humans, but instead serve a purpose. As Haselton et al. (2009) comment 'From an evolutionary perspective, however, it would be surprising if the mind were really so woefully muddled'. Instead, as discussed earlier, we use cognitive biases and heuristics to process the extensive amount of information that we are presented with as we engage with our environment, which includes our interactions with others. Those others are also making use of cognitive biases and heuristics, so not only must we understand our environment, but we must also account for the fact that the people we are interacting with will behave in ways which, on the surface, would appear to be irrational. Given this, it is not surprising that we make mistakes in navigating our social world. The key point as identified by Haselton et al. (2009) however is that we have evolved this system of heuristics and cognitive biases and continue because, more often than not, they provide us with an advantage. As will be discussed in greater detail in Chapter 6, this is something that should be recognised when attempts are being made to change human behaviour. In brief, behaviour change and prevention campaigns that aim to stop humans from making any use of heuristics and cognitive biases are very unlikely to be successful.

As noted by Workman (2008), many of the techniques used by social engineers are similar to those used within marketing. This is not perhaps surprising. Both social engineering and marketing are based on the principles of persuasion put forward by Cialdini (2001). For instance, Happ et al. (2016) explored the role of the social norm of reciprocity in social engineering, noting the norm of reciprocity is a very ingrained one. People will feel the need to return a favour, even if they did not invite the favour in the first place. Within cybersecurity this reciprocity can take the form of the exchange of information (Tamjidyamcholo, Bin Baba, Tamjid, & Gholipour, 2013). Other cognitive processes are exploited by social engineers, such as confirmation bias (Nickerson, 1998). Many phishing emails appear in formats that match what we would expect to see, such as the use of logos. This approach also utilises the representativeness heuristic (Kahneman & Tversky, 1972), in which we are more likely to judge something as legitimate if it is familiar. As several ethical social engineers have noted, these biases can be exploited in offline settings as well. For instance, wearing a high visibility jacket and other suitable clothing can be used to gain access to a site, with renowned ethical social engineer Jenny Radcliffe making use of this strategy to attend the Glastonbury music festival for free in her earlier days (Radcliffe, 2023).

Social engineers

Whilst the techniques used by social engineers have been studied (Mouton, Leenen, Malan, & Venter, 2014), there is limited research on social engineers. Instead, knowledge about the life experiences and characteristics of social engineers primarily comes directly from autobiographical accounts, which by their nature may be biased. There have been several books written by social engineers, including *Social Engineering: The Science of Human Hacking* (Hadnagy, 2018) and *People Hacker: Confessions of a Burglar for Hire* (Radcliffe, 2023), as well as popular podcasts that include interviews with social engineers, such as *Darknet Diaries* (Rhysider, 2017–). These sources provide valuable insights into the psyche of social engineers, but although some have re-labelled the discipline from an 'art' to a 'science' (Hadnagy, 2011, 2018), there remains a need for empirical research to better understand this population. Doing so will help inform prevention and mitigation strategies against social engineering attacks. It may also suggest ways in which people can be encouraged to consider ethical social engineering as a legitimate cybersecurity career path, which would help address the cybersecurity recruitment crises (ISACA, 2022). In support of this, it has been noted that many of the skills displayed by students from non-IT backgrounds, such as psychology, are especially relevant to the techniques typically used in social engineering attacks. This contrasts with the skillsets often displayed by students from IT backgrounds, whose education focuses more on technical aspects of cybersecurity (Taylor et al., 2017) rather than consideration of behaviour and more in depth analyses.

One of the challenges in understanding the role of social engineers in the cybercrime ecosystem is terminology. Hacking refers broadly to the act of using a system for a purpose other than what it was designed for. This does not in itself mean that the act of hacking is criminal, although it often has such connotations (Thackray, 2019). This concept of changing a system could be applied to socio-technical systems, and therefore include the human elements that are often targeted by social engineers. We would argue though that 'hacker' is typically used to mean an attack that is based on technological means and that social engineering is seen as a related but separate discipline. These blurred lines between different types of hacking activity reflect wider debates and discussions in the hacking community, which include whether 'hacker' is even a meaningful label (Thackray, Richardson, Dogan, Taylor, & McAlaney, 2017). These discussions are complicated by stereotypes and preconceptions of hackers, an issue that is not helped by conflicting results in the research literature. For example Woo (2003) observed high levels of narcissism and aggression in hackers, whereas Platt (1994) noted that, as a group, hackers appeared to be quite mild-mannered.

As outlined in the literature with reference to black hat and white hat hackers (McAlaney, Kimpton, & Thackray, 2019), there is also a distinction between those who commit acts of social engineering for criminal purposes (black hat) and those who do so for legitimate reasons (white hat). The latter is a form of penetration testing, in which for example a company may employ a social engineer to investigate the ease with which they could access sensitive data within that company. Again, there is inconsistent terminology used to describe this white hat approach to social engineering, but as noted earlier in this chapter, such individuals have been referred to as ethical social engineers. The stories in books written by high profile ethical social engineers such as Chris Hadnagy (2018) and Jenny Radcliffe (2023) demonstrate the ease with which a skilled social engineer is able to achieve their goal. A recurrent theme throughout these texts is that the target companies are often vastly overconfident in their ability to protect themselves against such attacks. It could be speculated this is because these organisations often equate a cybersecurity attack with a technological breach, rather than something that utilises trickery and psychological manipulation of the humans in the organisation. Indeed, these preconceptions held by individuals in the target company are often the very things used against that company by the social engineer.

As a starting point in understanding the life and motivation of ethical social engineers we can consider the work that has been done with hackers, albeit with an acknowledgement of the conflation between social engineering and hacking. The circumplex model by Seebruck (2015), discussed in more detail in Chapter 3, identifies five broad motivations for cybercrime – prestige, recreation, ideology, revenge, and profit. Of these, profit could feasibly be the most applicable to ethical social engineers, in that it is an activity that they receive payment for. However, from the accounts given in the media by ethical social engineers it would appear there are elements of prestige and recreation involved as well. Often, individuals talk about the sense of excitement they feel when, for instance, trying to gain access to a secure building, and the sense of accomplishment they feel when successful. Further there is an issue we would argue appears to be in the background when considering ethical social engineering that people are aware of, but which is rarely discussed – whether ethical social engineers have previously committed criminal acts. This has parallels with similar discussions in relation to hackers. As noted in previous research, companies will often state that they will not employ penetration testers who have a criminal record, and yet it appears to be an open secret that to be a successful white hat hacker requires at least some experience of criminal behaviour (Thackray, 2019). In other words, a successful white hat hacker may in fact be more of a grey hat hacker. From the accounts given by ethical social engineers in the media it would appear that many individuals have participated in actions that are likely illegal, particularly in their youth before they established themselves as an ethical social engineer (Rhysider, 2017–). Whilst many of the stories told by ethical social engineers suggest some criminality may have occurred (such as trespassing) there rarely appears to be any real criminal intent behind their actions; nevertheless, there may a reluctance for ethical social engineers to discuss in detail what experiences they have had. This is where academic research can contribute. It has been found for example that hackers will appear to speak relatively openly to academic researchers, provided that they trust the information they provide will be treated confidentially (Thackray et al., 2017).

Another avenue for understanding the experiences and characteristics of social engineers is forensic psychology. This discipline has been used to explore the identities and motivations of criminals, some of which may be applicable to both criminal and ethical social engineers. A challenge exists though in that, whilst social engineering includes offline activities, it typically also includes an online element. In discussing the role of forensic psychology in online spaces Kirwan and Power (2013) observe that there are two underlying assumptions often used in psychological profiling. Firstly, the consistency assumption, which states that offenders will exhibit similar behaviours throughout all their crimes (and allows for offences to be 'linked' to being undertaken by the same individual). Secondly, the homology assumption, states that similar offence styles tend to be associated with similar offender background characteristics (allowing for profiles of current offenders to be gleaned from what we know of previous offenders who have offended in similar ways). As Kirwan and Power (2013) comment there are some questions around the consistency assumption in relation to cybercrime; given how rapidly technology changes it may be assumed that methods used also change, although it has also been found that methods used by hacking groups can be consistent over several years (Preuß, Furnell, & Papadaki, 2007). Another potential difficulty with the consistency hypotheses is that although individuals or groups may behave consistently – they may all behave in similar ways – as such they may not be distinctive and therefore not easily distinguishable from one another in the methods they use. If hacking groups for example all use similar methods, then attributing which hacking group undertook which hack may be difficult. This could also be a difficulty for the homology hypothesis to cybercrime. If most hackers are well educated, young, white males with easy access to internet and specific computer software – as is the image that appears to be curated in some hacking forums (Thackray, 2019) – then regardless of similarities in their methods or offence style, the typical offender profile may be the same. It cannot distinguish between individuals. Moreover, a criticism levelled at more general profiling per se, is that profiles include mainly demographic rather than more nuanced personality or motivational aspects. The difficulty in gaining access to relevant data and the use of predominantly case studies due to lack of availability of large datasets from law enforcement has also been highlighted (Bada & Nurse, 2021). For example, their paper highlights 'action fraud UK' and also the National Fraud Database, which collect information in relation to victims, but there is no known database focusing on the collection of offender characteristics (Bada & Nurse, 2021). As such more research is required considering the different motives, skills, and contexts in which attacks take place to identify differences between different types of offenders (Bada & Nurse, 2021). However, Nykodym, Taylor, and Vilela (2005) argue that cybercrime profiling may be especially useful when dealing with insider threat, which in cybersecurity refers to employees who behave in ways that increase risk. This may be relevant to social engineering, which often involves manipulating employees within a company to behave in a way that unknowingly facilitates the attack. As such there could be potential for considering how the profile of ethical social engineers relates to the profile of those they target, so that a more holistic understanding of the situation can be reached.

Jenny Radcliffe's book *People Hacker: Confessions of a Burglar for Hire* outlines her life experiences as an ethical social engineer (Radcliffe, 2023). Radcliffe discusses how her interest in this career began as a young girl, when she would explore abandoned buildings in her hometown of Liverpool. This is an activity that would now be referred to as urban exploring, a hobby that is the basis of several popular YouTube channels. Radcliffe discusses the importance of having a plan, along with several backup plans, before attempting to access a building. In doing so she cites a near miss early in her career when an impulsive decision to start a job earlier than originally planned nearly resulted in her being caught and suffering a severe injury. This, and other discussions put forward by ethical social engineers, highlight the degree of preparation and planning that they put into a job. Indeed, it would often seem that they put in more effort than companies do to protect themselves. A common observation made by ethical social engineers is how they will by default try to open a door that, by all expectations, should be locked, on the basis that it is surprising how often this is not in fact the case. As Radcliffe highlights, security is often an illusion, pointing out for instance that many poorly fitted patio doors in homes can simply be lifted out of the frame, if the correct technique is used. Radcliffe also discusses how stereotypes and perceptions can aide her in her work. As she puts it, people do not expect a middle-aged woman to have any understanding of criminality. These misconceptions, coupled with overconfidence of the type that might perhaps be found amongst executives in large corporations, would seem to be a factor in why Radcliffe is so consistently successful in breaching their defences. To quote, 'I don't look at picking a lock. I look at the person whose job it is to keep the lock closed, then persuade them to open it.'

Physical lock picking is though not without its uses. In the *Darknet Diaries* episode 'The Deviant', the ethical penetration tester of the same pseudonym discusses his work on testing physical security as a service to companies (Rhysider, 2023). He also notes the ease with which this is often done, and often does not require any actual lock picking. When this is required, it typically poses little challenge as the interiors of wealthy companies with valuable information and products to protect are often secured behind inexpensive locks. A question that is raised in this podcast episode is why companies do not simply hire locksmiths to test their physical security, rather than professional penetration testers like Deviant. The response given in the interview is that part of the role of the professional penetration tester is to produce a report that explains to the company how they were able to gain access, but that the culture amongst professional locksmiths would be to treat these insights as protected knowledge. This issue of transparency in sharing how buildings and systems can be breached is a recurrent theme in cybersecurity. Sharing knowledge on different techniques is one of the main types of interaction on hacking forums (McAlaney, Hambidge, Kimpton, & Thackray, 2020), although it should be commented that this does not necessarily come with an endorsement that people then attempt to apply that technique themselves. Indeed, many times the tone of the discussion is how forum users – typically those with less experience – should *not* attempt to use these techniques, as they may be caught and prosecuted. Nevertheless, it is inevitable that some individuals will take this knowledge and attempt to use it for malicious purposes. As such, empowering people with knowledge on how cybercrimes are undertaken may give them greater insight and in turn a greater ability to protect themselves, but in doing so may also prompt others to explore cybercriminal activities in such ways.

References

Al-Ahmad, A. S., Kahtan, H., Hujainah, F., & Jalab, H. A. (2019). Systematic Literature Review on Penetration Testing for Mobile Cloud Computing Applications. *IEEE Access, 7*. doi:10.1109/ACCESS.2019.2956770

Almasy, S. (2016). Prank caller convinces Burger King workers to bust out windows. Retrieved from http://edition.cnn.com/2016/04/09/us/minnesota-burger-king-prank/index.html

Cialdini, R. B. (2001). *Influence: Science and Practice*. Boston, MA: Pearson Education.

Geer, D., & Harthorne, J. (2002, 9–13 Dec. 2002). *Penetration testing: a duet*. Paper presented at the 18th Annual Computer Security Applications Conference, 2002. Proceedings.

Hadnagy, C. (2011). *Social Engineering: The Art of Human Hacking*. Indianapolis, IN: Wiley Publishing Inc.

Hadnagy, C. (2018). *Social Engineering: The Science of Human Hacking*. Indianapolis, IN: Wiley.

Happ, C., Melzer, A., & Steffgen, G. (2016). Trick with treat - Reciprocity increases the willingness to communicate personal data. *Computers in Human Behavior, 61*, 372–377. doi:10.1016/j.chb.2016.03.026

Haselton, M. G., Bryant, G. A., Wilke, A., Frederick, D. A., Galperin, A., Frankenhuis, W. E., & Moore, T. (2009). ADAPTIVE RATIONALITY: AN EVOLUTIONARY PERSPECTIVE ON COGNITIVE BIAS. *Social Cognition, 27*(5), 733–763. doi:10.1521/soco.2009.27.5.733

Hasenstab, J. J. (2013). *Cyberbullying: A study of school administrators' perceptions and responses to online aggression*. (73). ProQuest Information & Learning, Retrieved from https://search.ebscohost.com/login.aspx?direct=true&db=psyh&AN=2013-99100-287&site=eds-live& scope=site Available from EBSCOhost psyh database.

ISACA. (2022). *State of Cybersecurity 2022: Global Update on Workforce Efforts, Resources and Cyberoperations*. Retrieved from https://www.isaca.org/go/state-of-cybersecurity-2022

Iuga, C., Nurse, J. R. C., & Erola, A. (2016). Baiting the hook: factors impacting susceptibility to phishing attacks. *Human-centric Computing and Information Sciences, 6*(1), 8. doi:10.1186/s13673-016-0065-2

Kahneman, D., & Tversky, A. (1972). Subjective probability: A judgment of representativeness. *Cognitive Psychology, 3*(3), 430–454. doi:https://doi.org/10.1016/0010-0285(72)90016-3

Kirwan, G., & Power, A. (2013). *Cybercrime: The Psychology of Online Offenders*. New York: Cambridge University Press.

McAlaney, J., Hambidge, S., Kimpton, E., & Thackray, H. (2020, 7–11 Sept. 2020). *Knowledge is power: An analysis of discussions on hacking forums.* Paper presented at the 2020 IEEE European Symposium on Security and Privacy Workshops (EuroS&PW).

McAlaney, J., Kimpton, E., & Thackray, H. (2019). *Fifty shades of grey hat: A socio-psychological analysis of conversations on hacking forums.* Paper presented at the CyPsy24, Norfolk, Virginia.

Mouton, F., Leenen, L., Malan, M. M., & Venter, H. S. (2014). *Towards an Ontological Model Defining the Social Engineering Domain.* Berlin: Heidelberg.

Nickerson, R. S. (1998). Confirmation Bias: A Ubiquitous Phenomenon in Many Guises. *Review of General Psychology, 2,* 175–220.

Northcraft, G. B., & Neale, M. A. (1987). Experts, amateurs, and real-estate – an anchoring-and-adjustment perspective on property pricing decisions. *Organizational Behavior and Human Decision Processes, 39*(1), 84–97. doi:10.1016/0749–5978(87)90046-x

Nykodym, N., Taylor, R., & Vilela, J. (2005). Criminal profiling and insider cyber crime. *Digital Investigation, 2*(4), 261–267. doi:10.1016/j.diin.2005.11.004

Platt, C. (1994). Hackers: threat or menace? *Wired, November 1994(2),* 82–88.

Preuß, J., Furnell, S. M., & Papadaki, M. (2007). Considering the potential of criminal profiling to combat hacking. *Journal in Computer Virology, 3*(2), 135–141. doi:10.1007/s11416-007-0042-4

Radcliffe, J. (2023). *People Hacker: Confessions of a Burglar for Hire.* London: Simon & Schuster.

Rhysider, J. (2017–). *Darknet Diaries.* Retrieved from https://darknetdiaries.com/

Rhysider, J. (2023). The Deviant. *Darknet Diaries.* Retrieved from https://darknetdiaries.com/

Ropek, L. (2022). Hackers Have Been Sending Malware-Filled USB Sticks to U.S. Companies Disguised as Presents. Retrieved from https://gizmodo.com/hackers-have-been-sending-malware-filled-usb-sticks-to-1848323578

Salahdine, F., & Kaabouch, N. (2019). Social engineering attacks: A survey. *Future Internet, 11*(4): 89.

Seebruck, R. (2015). A typology of hackers: Classifying cyber malfeasance using a weighted arc circumplex model. *Digital Investigation, 14,* 36–45. doi:http://dx.doi.org/10.1016/j.diin.2015.07.002

Tamjidyamcholo, A., Bin Baba, M. S., Tamjid, H., & Gholipour, R. (2013). Information security – Professional perceptions of knowledge-sharing intention under self-efficacy, trust, reciprocity, and shared-language. *Computers & Education, 68,* 223–232. doi:http://dx.doi.org/10.1016/j.compedu.2013.05.010

Taylor, J., McAlaney, J., Hodge, S., Thackray, H., Richardson, C., James, S., & Dale, J. (2017, 25–28 April 2017). *Teaching psychological principles to cybersecurity students.* Paper presented at the 2017 IEEE Global Engineering Education Conference (EDUCON).

Thackray, H. (2019). *Hackers gonna hack: Investigating the effect of group processes and social identities within online hacking communities.* PhD, Bournemouth University, Poole.

Thackray, H., Richardson, C., Dogan, H., Taylor, J., & McAlaney, J. (2017). *Surveying the hackers: The challenges of data collection from a secluded community.* Paper presented at the 16th European Conference on Cyber Warfare and Security, Dublin.

Woo, H. J. (2003). *The hacker mentality: exploring the relationship between psychological variables and hacking activities.* PhD, University of Georgia.

Workman, M. (2008). Wisecrackers: a theory-grounded investigation of phishing and pretext social engineering threats to information security. *Journal of the American Society for Information Science and Technology, 59.* doi:10.1002/asi.20779

Zhao, J., Shang, W., Wan, M., & Zeng, P. (2015, 8–12 June 2015). *Penetration testing automation assessment method based on rule tree.* Paper presented at the 2015 IEEE International Conference on Cyber Technology in Automation, Control, and Intelligent Systems (CYBER).

Attackers

3

Types and motivations of attackers

As commented by Chng, Lu, Kumar, and Yau (2022), the phrase 'hackers' has been used in the past in a way that suggests that hackers (or cybercriminals more broadly) consist of one generic group, which would be akin to considering all traditional criminals to have the same characteristics. Several taxonomies and typologies of cyber-attackers have been proposed within the literature. For example, Seebruck (2015) provides a circumplex model, within which attackers are classed as having a primary motivation of either prestige, recreation, revenge, ideology, or profit. Individual types of attackers exist within one of these segments, with varying degrees of technological skill. This highlights the point made in Chapter 1, that there is marked variation in how much technological skill hackers have (NCA, 2016), with less than 5% engaging in what would be considered to be sophisticated hacking (Holt & Bossler, 2014). This does not mean however that those lacking technological skills are low threat. As demonstrated in Chapter 2 psychological manipulation of targets, or social engineering, poses a significant threat but does not necessarily require technological ability. Technological skill is not also necessarily an indicator of the threat that a hacker poses, with Chua and Holt (2016) reporting that they did not find a relationship between technical computer skills and simpler forms of hacking, although there was such a relationship evident with regards to more complex forms of hacking. Similarly, it appears that higher technological skill is associated with stronger willingness to engage in website defacement, searching of bank or government servers, or the breaching of military servers (Bossler,

DOI: 10.4324/9781003300359-3

2019; Holt, Freilich, & Chermak, 2017; Holt, Kilger, Chiang, & Yang, 2016; Holt, Kilger, Chiang, & Yang, 2015).

Several of the segments identified in Seebruck's model are ones which the public are likely to be familiar with, others less so. The profit segment for example includes those attackers who engage in hacking for financial gain, such as those who use various means to fraudulently access bank accounts or credit cards. Hacktivists on the other hand commit cyber-attacks for ideological purposes, such as in protest against companies or governments who they deem to be acting in an amoral way (Hutchings, 2013). The first documented case of a DDoS being conducted for a hacktivist cause was by Italian artists in 1995, who brought down some French government websites in protest against nuclear testing that France was involved in (Milan, 2015). One of the hacktivist groups people are most likely to be aware of is Anonymous, who rose to prominence in the late 2000s and early 2010s through a series of high-profile incidents, including conflict with the Church of Scientology (Knappenberger, 2012). The group is known for the adoption of a Guy Fawkes mask as its symbol, an image that comes from the graphic novel *V for Vendetta* (Moore, 1982–1989), later made into a movie of the same name in 2005. Anonymous are notable as a hacktivist group as their initial online activities led to offline meetings and activities, including The Million Mask March, held on the 5th of November each year – the date on which Guy Fawkes attempted to destroy the House of Lords in the UK (BBC News, 2016). More recently, Anonymous has conducted attacks against the invasion of Ukraine, including disabling the Russian state news website (Purtill, 2022). In the style of trolling typical to Anonymous, the collective also appeared to hack electrical vehicle charging station screens in Russia to display messages such as 'Glory to Ukraine'. Bradshaw and Howard (2018) note that low barriers to entry and reduced communication costs afforded by social media are often assumed to have changed the balance of power for minor political players. This is reflected in many ways such as terrorist recruitment and coordination (Bernard, 2017), the increased disruption that can be caused by marginal social movements (Owen, 2015), and the actions of hacktivist collectives such as Anonymous (Coleman, 2014).

Some of the other hacker types identified in Seebruck's model may be less familiar to the public. Revenge refers to the situation where an individual commits or facilitates a cyber-attack in response to perceived mistreatment from another. This type of threat is often considered in relation to disgruntled employees and is discussed further in Chapter 6, as part of organisational culture. Both prestige and recreation are lesser-known reasons for engagement in hacking but can be powerful motivators. In keeping with the motivation of prestige, it has been noted that one of the main themes of the discussions held on hacking forums is knowledge, in which users share expertise and provide opinions on all hacking related topics (Thackray, 2019). This reflects the fact that hacking exists as a subculture (Holt, 2007; Steinmetz, 2014). Within these hacking forums there is competition to be the most knowledgeable and the most skilled. Part of this is the enjoyment that individuals experience from hacking, which highlights that hacking can be done as a recreational activity. Steinmetz (2014) reports a range of emotions that hackers experience whilst going through the hacking process, including frustration and boredom, with pleasure and euphoria experienced when a hack is completed. It is important to note that, as with all cases of hacking, hacking for recreation does not necessarily mean that the hacking being conducted is criminal in nature. Hacking as a recreation may be something that people engage in throughout their lives. Despite the stereotype of hackers being teenagers, people who engage in hacking have a wide age range (Thackray, Richardson, Dogan, Taylor, & McAlaney, 2017). Those individuals who may have begun hacking in their youth in the 1980s and 1990s are now older and may be in in legitimate full-time employment with families, community work and other commitments that often come with middle-age but continue to hack for the pleasure in doing so. Hacking for recreation overlaps with attacking a target because the attackers consider it amusing to do so, which in the parlance of hacking forum discussions is referred to as doing it for the lulz (Olson, 2012). Another common motivator for engagement in hacking appears to be curiosity (Hutchings, 2013; McAlaney, Hambidge, Kimpton, & Thackray, 2020), in that hackers navigate the internet and computer systems due to their interest in these systems, rather than due to any desire to commit criminal actions. This relates to the concept of digital drift as discussed in Chapter 1, in which people may feel that mainstream norms do not apply on the internet. It also reflects the life experiences reported by social engineers, as discussed in Chapter 2, who often describe how they began their social engineering activities through a desire to explore an unknown environment.

There is evidence that supports the view that the actions of different types of hacker match how they identify and describe themselves. For example, it has been noted that hacktivists are more likely to target websites that are antithetical to their own views (such as targeting large corporations who the hacktivists believe behave amorally) than they are to hack for curiosity or financial purposes (Holt et al., 2017; Holt et al., 2016). The exact motivations of hackers can, however, be difficult to identify, in part due to what can sometimes appear to be contrasting actions and attitudes. For example, following a hack of a cryptocurrency, hackers returned nearly half of the $600 million that they stole (Kharpal & Browne, 2021). Similarly, it was reported that a ransomware gang apologised to a children's hospital and provided them with decryption software (Abrams, 2023). It would seem that online attackers have their own sets of standards and beliefs about what is not acceptable. This is akin to the 'moral code' witnessed in broader criminality where stealing from a large company may be seen as more acceptable than robbing an elderly female; or where murdering a bank employee in an armed robbery is viewed as far more 'acceptable' than sexually abusing and killing a child. Chiesa, Ducci, and Ciappi (2008) further describe hackers in terms of the belief that systems which have been breached should not be damaged, that data should not be stolen or modified, that information should be shared with other members of the hacking community, and that access to the system should be given to all. This is consistent with research that has found that people who identify as hackers have mixed opinions on what is acceptable in terms of hacking, although it has been noted there is greater consensus on the view that cybersecurity gaps should be exposed, if not exploited (Thackray et al., 2017). This reflects the frustrations often expressed by hackers how large organisations can have basic gaps in their cybersecurity (Chua & Holt, 2016), despite having the resources to easily address these issues (Goode & Cruise, 2006). Further, there are complex relationships between motivation, belief systems, the type of hacker, and the type of attack committed. For instance, Holt et al. (2015) found that a perception that there are clear rules on what is acceptable online is predictive of being less likely to engage in website defacement, but was not predictive of other types of cyber-attack. Similarly, a belief that individuals should be able to view any information about them that is held by government, school, or business was found to be predictive of viewing website defacement and accessing government servers, but not predictive of a view that it is ok to compromise military servers.

Chng et al. (2022) propose a further framework for hacker types, motivation, and strategies, echoing the point that cybersecurity research to date has focussed more on the technological aspects of cybersecurity than the human element. The framework overlaps with Seebruck's (2015) circumplex model but suggests additional types of hacker including old guards (established and experienced hackers), insiders (internal members of an organisation), petty thieves, crowdsources, and crime facilitators. Crime facilitators relate to CaaS, as discussed in Chapter 1. The model deliberately does not include the older term of cracker, identified by Barber (2001) and used to refer to hackers who intentionally cause damage, on the basis that this is a broad concept that could be applied to several types of hacker. Chng et al. (2022) note that the terms they use reflect the terms used in the cybercommunity, and identify further terms that have been used in the literature, including nation states (Hald & Pedersen, 2012) and online sex offenders (Donalds & Osei-Bryson, 2014) as cybercriminal types. The latter inclusion is interesting. Even on forums and sites that identify themselves as being opposed to mainstream society there is often a quick and severe response to anyone who appears to be endorsing or seeking child pornography (Coleman, 2014).

Identifying motivations of hackers is more difficult by conflicting reports and research studies into the personality and demeanour of those involved in hacking. For example Woo (2003) observed high levels of narcissism and aggression in hackers, whereas Platt (1994) noted that as a group hackers appeared to be quite amiable. Similarly, Bachmann (2010) states hackers appear to prefer rational thinking styles and problem solving, which contrasts the image – albeit one often curated by hacking group themselves – of hackers as unpredictable anarchists (Coleman, 2014). This perception of hackers as socially maladjusted malcontents is perhaps partly due to the way in which hackers sometimes interact with each other. When looking online at discussions around hacking and hacktivism, it is evident that many users communicate in an aggressive way (Olson, 2012). However, this may just be the way in which those groups communicate. Online interactions have been characterised as being prone to several specific interpretations. For example, Poe's Law has been described as an adage that any parodic or sarcastic statement made online will be taken as sincere, unless the author's intent is made explicitly clear (Aikin, 2009). Nevertheless, in some cases it does seem that cyberattacks on some individuals and organisations are a case of displaced aggression (Pedersen, Bushman, Vasquez, & Miller, 2008). Motivations can also be fluid, and different members of the same group or collective have differing and sometimes conflicting motivations for being involved in attacks. For instance, the distinction between targeting an organisation to address a perceived social injustice and doing it for personal enjoyment (i.e. for the lulz) became a reason for in-group conflict in Anonymous (Coleman, 2014). In addition, more than one motivation may be present in the same individual. Whilst the members of Anonymous could be considered to be primarily motivated by hacktivism, it has been reported that some members of the group also engaged in credit card fraud as a means of income (Coleman, 2014). Of course, caution should also be taken when categorising hackers based on self-report of their identity and motivations. Presenting oneself as an ideologically motivated hacker fighting the greed of a large corporation is more socially acceptable than simply being a criminal who steals money. This reflects the observation by Rogers (2010) that those who do engage in cybercrime cope with the cognitive dissonance this creates in four ways:

- Through using euphemistic language that minimises and distances their actions
- Blaming their actions on social pressures and claiming that, in the case of group actions, their individual contribution was minimal
- Minimising or disregarding the negative consequences of their actions
- Vilifying and dehumanising their targets, and stating that they deserved to be attacked

Finally, there is the stereotype of hackers as being socially inept or being more likely than members of the general population to be on the autism scale. Such stereotypes should be viewed with some criticality. Rogers (2010) points out that social skills can take many forms, and people who may not be socially adept offline can be extremely socially skilled online. The social networks evident on hacking forums are complex and nuanced (McAlaney et al., 2020), and those hackers who make use of social engineering techniques both offline and online demonstrate extremely good social skills. Still, there continues to be debate on whether hackers are more likely than others to be experiencing a psychological disorder than the general population, and if so whether it is the presence of this disorder which leads to the individual becoming involved in hacking. Kirwan and Power (2013) argue that three factors are typically considered when determining if an offender is displaying a psychological disorder – discomfort, dysfunction, and deviance, which they note can be difficult to apply to real world examples. Discomfort refers to whether the individual is experiencing distress that could be a contributory factor to their behaviour. If they are not experiencing such discomfort, but are behaving in an abnormal way, then this could be an indicator of a psychological disorder. Similarly, if they are experiencing discomfort, but do not show signs of psychological distress, then this would also often be considered to be abnormal. Whether this can be applied to cybercriminals is complex. For example, a hacktivist who feels discomfort at the actions of a large multi-national company may use hacking techniques to cause harm to that company. In doing so they are exhibiting a behaviour that is intended to decrease their discomfort, but the behaviour in question is an illegal one. Dysfunction refers to if a person can manage their daily life effectively. As noted, whilst some hackers may not engage fully with mainstream society, they can often have rich and extensive social relationships with others in the hacking world. In the case of cybercriminals, they also use their skills and knowledge to generate an income – albeit an illegal one. Finally, deviance refers to any form of unusual behaviour. This is again a difficult concept to easily apply to cybercrime, as it requires consensus on what qualifies as a normal behaviour. Technology evolves rapidly, and the online behaviours of someone with an interest in digital technologies may seem very unusual to someone who does not understand those technologies. For instance, the now ethical hacker Kevin Mitnick was imprisoned in his younger years in which it was erroneously claimed by the prosecution in his court case that he 'could launch nuclear weapons by whistling into a payphone' (Burkeman, 2002). Overall, there are as many challenges in determining if cybercriminals exhibit any form of psychological disorder as those who commit traditional crimes.

One potential avenue to better understand cybercriminals is to apply research into profiling, as has been done in forensic psychology to traditional forms of crime. Nykodym, Taylor, and Vilela (2005) argue that cybercrime profiling may be especially useful when dealing with insider threat, which refers to employees or members of an organisation acting in ways to facilitate cybercrime intentionally or unintentionally. This potential for increased profiling with members of an organisation is due to the increased information that is available in an organisation as opposed to within public settings, as organisations are typically able to monitor the device usage of their members more closely. This will be discussed in greater detail in Chapters 5 and 6. One larger scale attempt to profile hackers was the Hackers Profiling Project (Chiesa et al., 2008). This work used a variety of data collection means, including direct surveying of individuals who identified as engaging in hacking. The authors note that the image of a 'hacker' is a blurry one but do identify some commonalities from the data they collected. This included the observation that hackers are generally intelligent, creative, and resolute, with a high sense of curiosity and a desire to find new ways of approaching challenges. This is consistent with work by McAlaney et al. (2020), who found that hackers appear to be primarily driven by a wish to understand online technologies and to test their boundaries, rather than by any fundamental desire to commit crime. Chiesa et al. (2008) also report that there are mixed motivations for engaging with hackers, and a range of value systems on who it is acceptable to target for cyber-attack. This is consistent with the work of Seebruck (2015), and illustrates the complexity of hacker identity and the challenges in attempting to construct profiles that can summarise hacker attitudes and behaviours. It is telling that hackers themselves express frustration with the term 'hacker', on the basis that it covers such a broad range of activities and identities to be meaningless (Thackray et al., 2017). This reflects wider frustrations that hackers have with stereotypes and media portrayals of hacking – such as the infamous scene from the television show *NCIS* dubbed by the hacking community as 'Two idiots, one keyboard' in which two characters attempt to prevent a cyber-attack in progress by simultaneously typing on the same computer keyboard. This scene may have been an attempt to portray the concept of flow, which appears to be a popular concept when hackers and cybersecurity professionals are depicted in the media. Flow refers to a sense of effortless action that is felt when an individual is completely engaged in a task, and lose track of time and awareness of external distractions (Csikszentmihalyi, 1990) – a state described in sports for example as being in the zone. Beveren (2001) argues that the flow state is part of the reason why people become involved in hacking, and further divides hacker motivation into four themes: i) compulsion to hack, ii) curiosity, iii) control and attraction, and iv) peer recognition and belonging to a group. Further, Beveren (2001) suggests that flow can occur in hacking when the hacker: i) perceives they have control over the interaction, ii) the hacker is paying full attention to the interactions, iii) the hacker is experiencing curiosity about the interaction, and iv) the hacker finds the interaction to be intrinsically interesting. Again, it is difficult to evaluate theories such as this one against the reality of how hackers behave and communicate given the nature of the population. However, concepts of control and being in a flow state (albeit with the acknowledgment that this is not a phrase hackers themselves may use) would appear to be evident from the interactions that can be observed on hacking forums.

Group processes

Hackers often begin by working on their own (Jones & Carroll, 2007), but soon develop relationships with other hackers (Schell & Dodge, 2002). As discussed in Chapter 1, this can include participation in cybercriminal gangs and the wider cybercrime ecosystem. Most research on attackers within the cybersecurity space focuses on hackers, and to a lesser extent, social engineers. However, there are other types of cyber-attacks, such as online harassment and bullying. Cyberspace has been described from the early days of the internet as a network of networks, highlighting how both processes within and between groups can shape individual behaviour (Hughes, 1994). It has been established that associating with deviant peers is one of the strongest predictors of engagement in crime, both traditional crime (Pratt et al., 2010) and cybercrime (Holt, Burruss, & Bossler, 2010). This is consistent with social psychological research, in which it has been observed that being a member of a group can influence an individual in several ways. People will tend to alter their behaviour and cognitions to match the group (Kelman, 2006), which may be a factor in why hacking groups, particularly hacktivists, act collectively against the same target. Online groups can also develop their own language and norms that are used to signal membership (Dobusch & Schoeneborn, 2015), which is evident in the use of jargon, argot, and memes within hacking groups (Coleman, 2014). Emotions can spread through a group to an individual, even if the individual was not involved in the original situation that caused that emotion (Smith, Seger, & Mackie, 2007). This is again something that has been documented in hacking groups, especially hacktivist collectives (Coleman, 2014). In those cases, the shared emotion that spreads through the group is often a sense of anger at a perceived injustice, such as businesses acting in an unethical manner. People are also more likely to conform to the viewpoints of others when they are in novel or uncertain situations (Spears, 2021). This could be argued to often be the case with cybercriminal activities, where some group members – especially those who are younger, or less experienced in hacking – may not fully understand the situation they are becoming involved in. However, relying on a group to determine the best action to take in an uncertain situation may not be wise. Individuals are known to make riskier decisions when in groups than when alone (Wallach, Kogan, & Bem, 1962), but at the same time people also tend to underestimate how much they are being influenced by the group (Darley, 1992). Whilst there is limited research in this area, it could be expected that people who become involved in hacking are especially vulnerable to underestimating how much they are influenced by others. The rhetoric used amongst hacking forums often tends to be framed in terms of the hacker being an individual with anarchist qualities who is anti-Establishment. Somewhat counterintuitively, anonymity can also increase one's sense of membership in online groups (Tanis & Postmes, 2005). Caution should be taken however in making assumptions about participation in group-based cybercriminal activities. For example, police in Kazakhstan arrested a gang who were found to be forcing IT specialists to run cryptocurrency farms (Tassev, 2022).

The category differentiation model (Doise, 1978) suggests that identifying groups as being such (categories) can strengthen the sense of group membership. We may have different roles as 'friend', 'parent', 'employee', 'sports team member', etc. and in each group we may play different parts to varying degrees. In each however we will have a different identity. Based on social identity theory, the subjective group dynamics model suggests that people may derive self-esteem from the groups to which they belong (Marques, Abrams, & Serodio, 2001). This is clearly demonstrated in street gangs where the gang may act as a surrogate-family purporting to provide peer acceptance, security, respect, and support from within (the in-group) and potentially inciting fear from others (the out-group) – although often the anticipated protection does not materialise (Levell, 2022). Interestingly, 'initiation' challenges individuals are asked to complete in order to be accepted and join a gang (to become part of the in-group) – such as injure someone, or take a beating (Murer & Schwarze, 2022) – are an extreme, yet similar idea to 'challenges' used in order for individuals to gain access to restricted sites and forums (e.g. on the dark web) – such as knowing how to post a correctly formatted Triforce sign, an image that is associated with the Legend of Zelda videogame series (Bernstein et al., 2011). However, participation in cyber groups and their related criminal activities might not be voluntary. If, as discussed, individuals who get involved in hacking become immersed in the social world of hacking forums and communications then this sense of social identity may be an important source of self-esteem. This is something that should be considered when attempts are being made to prevent people from becoming involved in cybercriminal activities. Being part of that group may be very important to that individual and removing that source of social support from them could have unintended consequences. It has been observed that most discussions that take place on surface web hacking forums stress to forum members – especially younger and less experienced hackers – that they should not engage in illegal activities (McAlaney et al., 2020). The rhetoric used amongst hacking forums often tends to be framed in terms of the hacker being an individual with anarchist qualities who is anti-Establishment (Coleman, 2014). This may reinforce the affinity that group members feel with their hacking group, as it further signifies the idea of the group being distinct from mainstream society. Nevertheless, there are also cases where it has been alleged that group members have manipulated less experienced hackers into committing cybercrime without that individual fully understanding what they are doing or being able to provide an informed defence of their actions when identified by law enforcement. For instance, in the documentary *We Are Legion* it is suggested that less knowledgeable members of the hacktivist collective Anonymous were manipulated into taking the blame for cyber-attacks against the Church of Scientology (Knappenberger, 2012). As identified by Deutsch & Gerard (1955) we are subject to both informational and normative influence, which means that we are driven to conform based on a desire to be accepted by a group, and to accept the version of reality put forward by that group. As such, people become part of hacking groups and take part in actions that they would not have otherwise done, particularly if they are being actively targeted and moulded by other group members.

Cybercriminal networks have important social dependency relationships (Leukfeldt, Kleemans, & Stol, 2017). Nurse and Bada (2019) observe that, despite being primarily identified as cybercriminal gangs, there does often appear to be a degree of offline interaction between members. Hacking groups also appear to be highly reliant on a sense of trust between members. Intergroup conflict can have a strong influence on the behaviour and self-identity of a group. In 2011 Aaron Barr, an executive at a digital security company called HBGary, decided to demonstrate his skills by infiltrating Anonymous (Olson, 2012). His intention was to reveal the real-world identity of the group members, known as doxing, although it was later found that he had misidentified several members. This prompted Anonymous to target Aaron Barr, and in doing so were able to hack into the HBGary company system. This allowed them to identify Barr's password, which they also ascertained was the password for his Facebook, Twitter, Yahoo and World of Warcraft accounts. The group then hijacked Barr's social media account and posted various embarrassing comments, including quotes from his emails. In psychological terms this could be described as removing Barr's ability to impression manage (Goffman, 1959), as in controlling how he was seen by the world. Anonymous then released Barr's home address, social security number and mobile phone number, after which he became subject to an escalating series of attacks. The attacks only began to cease after an appeal from Barr's wife, who spoke about the distress that the situation was causing herself and their children (Olson, 2012). This conflict with an external threat appeared to reinforce Anonymous' sense of cohesion and identity, and as such had the opposite effect of that intended by Barr – rather than disrupting the group he caused them to act more cohesively and efficiently. In much the same way that we make attributions at an individual level it has also been suggested that we may make intergroup attributions (Hewstone & Jaspars, 1982). This could include attributing the success of the groups to the skills and abilities of the members and attributing the success of the other group to external factors and luck. This could partly account for the confidence that Barr felt when he believed that he could successfully infiltrate Anonymous. It may also explain why members of Anonymous in turn felt safe in retaliating against Barr, in that they perceived themselves to be more skilled. Whilst this may indeed have been the case, these members still exposed themselves to risk, with several individuals later being arrested for their actions (Olson, 2012).

The case of the conflict between HBGary and Anonymous – and the numerous other examples of conflict between hacking groups, individuals, organisations and other hacking groups – involves several psychological processes. Given that most of the conflict happens online it is possible that a degree of disinhibition is present, which refers to how actions taken online do not feel as real to individuals as actions taken offline (Suler, 2004). This may prompt individuals to act more aggressively than they would if they were engaging with that person face to face – a tendency otherwise known as being a keyboard warrior. Deindividuation may also be a factor, which refers to how individuals may have a reduced sense of individuality and autonomy when in a group, although it has been observed that this can be a complex and unpredictable phenomenon (Reicher, Spears, & Postmes, 1995). Perceived social norms may be a further factor in shaping hacker group behaviour. Social norms, in one form or another, are an element of several broad psychological theories of behaviour, including the Theory of Planned Behaviour (Ajzen, 1991) and social learning theories (Bandura, 1986). They are the perceptions and beliefs that we hold about those around us. This aspect of perception is an important one to note, as research has demonstrated that people often misperceive social norms, with a tendency towards assuming their peers behave and think in ways that are substantially more socially irresponsible than is the case (McAlaney, Bewick, & Hughes, 2011). These misperceptions could in part also be fuelled by minority influence, in which an individual is able to convince a group to adhere to the individual's views and decisions, in contrast to the more expected process where the individual conforms to the group (Wood, Lundgren, Ouellette, Busceme, & Blackstone, 1994). This can occur when the individual concerned is consistent and adamant in their view, which prompts the group to consider that the individual must be correct. In other words, people are aware that the norm is to conform to a group opinion, so if they witness someone defying this social convention, they assume that they are doing so for a good reason. Reflecting this, it has been observed that individuals who appear to be confident in their opinions will argue against group consensus on hacking forums (McAlaney et al., 2020). Whether or not such individuals are correct in their views is, of course, another question. Overall, the conflicts that hacking and cybercriminal groups become involved in appear to be very in keeping with the type of conflicts studied throughout social psychology, such as the famous Robber Cave experiment by Sherif in the 1950s, in which two groups of boys were manipulated into exhibiting inter-group conflict (Sherif, White, & Harvey, 1955).

In a further example of intergroup conflict, hackers have been observed to target other hacking groups due to their objections about how that other group operates. For example, it has been reported the online harassment and stalking forum Kiwi Farms discussed later in the chapter has been hacked, with the personal information of users released (Holt, 2022). This appeared to prompt some intragroup conflict, with users of the forum expressing their anger at the forum founder, Joshua Moon. The identity and motivation of the hackers are not known, but it could be commented that the act of doxing individuals from a forum who pride themselves on harassing people with doxing is something that would very much appeal to certain hacking groups. More broadly, hackers may target others because they exist in another country or culture that the hacker perceives to be somehow inferior, or amoral. It has been reported for instance that individuals express more willingness to hack and cause harm to foreign governments than their own (Bossler, 2021). This relates to the concept of patriotic hackers, which are groups or individuals who target foreign governments and organisations who they perceive to be in conflict with their home country (Dahan, 2013).

Whilst hackers, and particularly hacktivists, are often involved in intergroup conflicts with external organisations of certain types there are other groups who focus their cyberaggression at more specific targets. This includes extremist groups who, despite being characterised by views that are as far part as it is possible to be, typically share xenophobic beliefs that there is a threat posed by specific ethnic, racial, or religious groups (Perry & Blazak, 2010). T. J. Holt, J. D. Freilich, and S. M. Chermak (2017) argue that members of these groups are under pressure to quickly demonstrate their adherence to the movement, partly due to their awareness of their conflict with that of mainstream society and the risk of infiltration by law enforcement agents. However, individuals lack the same options to signify group membership that are available in face-to-face interactions. As such there is a greater reliance on using unique language within the groups, known as argot. This type of argot can be very evidence in some online groups, such as discussion on incel forums. Incel forum users are assumed to be primarily male heterosexuals, but as noted in the literature there is some uncertainty over this (Jaki et al., 2019). Sugiura (2021) identifies the extensive vocabulary used within incel forums, which include Chads (the antithesis of an incel; a man who is sexually successful with women), Femoid (a dehumanising term for women), JBW (just be white, a belief that women will primarily choose white males as romantic or sexual partners), and Truecel (a true incel, one who has never touched a woman and is unable to have sex). Those who identify as an incel on these forums further distinguish themselves from mainstream society by discussing having taken the red pill (amongst other colour variations) and awoken to the 'reality' that women run the world and that they themselves will never be able to have a romantic or sexual relationship with a woman. The term 'red pill' comes from a community initially established on Reddit, which itself was a reference to the famous scene in the 1999 film *The Matrix*, in which Keanu Reeves' character is asked to choose between taking two pills – a blue pill, which will allow him to continue in his fake, simulated life, or a red pill that will show him the real world.

A related phenomenon is the harassment of online figures and communities. One of the more well-known online forums that facilitated this harassment was Kiwi Farms, which has previously been known as CWCki Forums. This community organised group trolling and talking, and doxed (revealed the real-world identity) of online personalities. It also targeted women, LGBTQIA+ people, and neurodivergent people. This included some instances of harassment in offline settings (Pless, 2016). The group made use of tragedies such as the mass shootings in two mosques in Christchurch, New Zealand, in 2019 as the basis for their trolling and harassment. The actions of the group have been alleged to be a factor in the suicide of three individuals (Dress, 2022). Causing individuals to commit suicide was one of the stated aims to the group, with a counter of deaths they felt responsible for visible on their website (Veale, 2020). The forum was removed from the internet by several internet providers who objected to its content, although at the time of writing it has been able to regain an online presence.

Intragroup conflict can also shape the actions of a group. This is exemplified by the revelation that a senior member of Anonymous was an informant for the FBI, which appeared to do extensive damage to the group (Coleman, 2014). Cybercriminal networks of the type discussed in Chapter 1 also have important social dependency relationships (Leukfeldt et al., 2017), with hacking groups also appearing to be highly reliant on a sense of trust between members (Thackray & McAlaney, 2018). Nurse and Bada (2019) observe that, despite being cybercriminals, there does often appear to be a degree of offline interactions between members. This supports the argument the relationships between hackers and cybercriminals should not be seen as less valid or meaningful than offline relationships just because the interactions primarily take place online. These groups appear to experience the same full range or group processes and conflicts as have been recorded in offline groups. Indeed, it has been commented by cybercrime investigators that hacker 'drama' can be leveraged to coax group members into revealing information that can then be used by law enforcement to identify and arrest group members (Troia, 2020). This type of conflict and drama are perhaps not surprising, considering the constraints that such groups must operate under when compared to offline criminal groups. This includes difficulties in in confirming the identity of their collaborators and limits to the enforcement of agreements, partly because threats of physical violence may not be applicable in the online environment (Dupont & Lusthaus, 2022; Lusthaus, 2018). As discussed by Lusthaus, Kleemans, Leukfeldt, Levi, and Holt (2023), it appears that cybercriminals have developed various strategies to attempt to overcome these barriers. This includes using closed forums, having new members be vouched for by existing members, and for new members to provide evidence such as stolen credit card details to prove they are an active cybercriminal (Dupont, Côté, Boutin, & Fernandez, 2017; Holt, Smirnova, Chua, & Copes, 2015; Soudijn & Zegers, 2012; Yip, Webber, & Shadbolt, 2013). It has been noted however that these strategies do not always appear to be effective, with for instance members who lacked the requisite skillset being nevertheless able to gain access to the notorious dark web forum marketplace Darkode (Dupont et al., 2017). Cases such as this one demonstrate a fundamental conflict experienced by cybercriminal forums and marketplaces – they need to promote their services and recruit new members, but also wish to avoid infiltration by law enforcement officials and competitors with malicious intent.

The interconnectedness of the cybercriminal ecosystem provides opportunities for research and investigation. Lu, Luo, Polgar, and Cao (2010) demonstrated for example how social network analysis could be applied to understanding the characteristics of one hacker network called Shadowcrew. They noted the presence of cliques in the network, with some members more involved in sub-groups than others. They also observed that despite being a decentralised network, members of Shadowcrew do not have equal status. Instead, different roles and power levels were evident, such as administrators, reviewers, moderators, vendors, and general members, indicating elaborate divisions of labour. This is similar to a team organisation structure, as defined by Best and Luckenbill (1994). Other techniques have been used to study the cybercrime ecosystem include interviewing offenders and investigators (Hutchings & Clayton, 2016; Lusthaus, 2018), victim surveys (Williams, Levi, Burnap, & Gundur, 2019), analysis of cybercriminal marketplaces and forums (Décary-Hétu & Dupont, 2012; Dupont et al., 2017) and employing data science and machine learning to collect data from cybercriminal settings (Pastrana, Thomas, Hutchings, &

Clayton, 2018). Lusthaus et al. (2023) identified several characteristics of cyber-criminal networks through case-studied analysis of ten closed investigations. This study documented varying types of types of network structure within the groups involved in the case studies, with some being characterised by looser group structure and less-defined roles, and with others having a clearer hierarchy and allocation of duties. Offline elements were evident across many of the chosen case studies, highlighting the point that there is not always a clear division between cybercrime and traditional, offline crimes. As technology becomes increasingly pervasive in daily life it is important that we continue to consider this interaction between offline and online components of what we may have otherwise considered to be cybercrime.

References

Abrams, L. (2023). Ransomware gang apologizes, gives SickKids hospital free decryptor. Retrieved from https://www.bleepingcomputer.com/news/security/ransomware-gang-apologizes-gives-sickkids-hospital-free-decryptor/amp/

Aikin, S. (2009). Poe's Law, Group Polarization, and the Epistemology of Online Religious Discourse. *SSRN Electronic Journal.* doi:10.2139/ssrn.1332169

Aitken, S., Gaskell, D., & Hodkinson, A. (2018). Online Sexual Grooming: Exploratory Comparison of Themes Arising From Male Offenders' Communications with Male Victims Compared to Female Victims. *Deviant Behavior, 39*(9), 1170–1190. doi:10.1080/01639625.2017.1410372

Ajzen, I. (1991). The theory of planned behaviour. *Organizational Behavior and Human Decision Processes, 50,* 179–211.

Bachmann, M. (2010). The risk propensity and rationality of computer hackers. *International Journal of Cyber Criminology, 4*(1–2), 642–656.

Bandura, A. (1986). *Social Foundations for Thought and Action.* Englewood Cliffs, N.J.: Prentice Hall.

Barber, R. (2001). Hackers Profiled — Who Are They and What Are Their Motivations? *Computer Fraud & Security, 2001,* 14–17. doi:10.1016/S1361-3723(01)02017-6

BBC News. (2016). Police make 53 arrests at the Million Mask March. Retrieved from https://www.bbc.co.uk/news/uk-england-london-37886876

Bernard, R. (2017). These are not the terrorist groups you're looking for: an assessment of the cyber capabilities of Islamic State. *Journal of Cyber Policy, 2*(2), 255–265. doi:10.1080/23738871.2017.1334805

Bernstein, M., Monroy-Hernández, A., Harry, D., André, P. A., Panovich, K., & Vargas, G. (2011). *4chan and /b/: An Analysis of Anonymity and Ephemerality in a Large Online Community.*

Best, J., & Luckenbill, D. (1994). *Organizing deviance* (2nd edn). Englewood Cliffs, N.J.: Prentice Hall.

Beveren, J. V. (2001). *A CONCEPTUAL MODEL OF HACKER DEVELOPMENT AND MOTIVATIONS. Journal of E-Business, 1*(2).

Bossler, A. M. (2019). Perceived formal and informal sanctions on the willingness to commit cyber attacks against domestic and foreign targets. *Journal of Crime and Justice, 42*(5), 599–615. doi:10.1080/0735648X.2019.1692423

Bossler, A. M. (2021). Neutralizing Cyber Attacks: Techniques of Neutralization and Willingness to Commit Cyber Attacks. *American Journal of Criminal Justice, 46*(6), 911–934. doi:10.1007/s12103-021-09654-5

Bradshaw, S., & Howard, P. N. (2018). THE GLOBAL ORGANIZATION OF SOCIAL MEDIA DISINFORMATION CAMPAIGNS. *Journal of International Affairs, 71*(1.5), 23–32. Retrieved from https://www.jstor.org/stable/26508115

Burkeman, O. (2002, 13/12/2002). 'Why did I do it? For fun'. *The Guardian*. Retrieved from https://www.theguardian.com/technology/2002/dec/13/g2.usnews

Chiesa, R., Ducci, S., & Ciappi, S. (2008). *Profiling Hackers: The Science of Criminal Profiling as Applied to the World of Hacking*: Auerbach Publications.

Chng, S., Lu, H. Y., Kumar, A., & Yau, D. (2022). Hacker types, motivations and strategies: A comprehensive framework. *Computers in Human Behavior Reports, 5*, 100167. doi:https://doi.org/10.1016/j.chbr.2022.100167

Chua, Y. T., & Holt, T. (2016). A Cross-National Examination of the Techniques of Neutralization to Account for Hacking Behaviors. *Victims & Offenders, 11*, 1–22. doi:10.1080/15564886.2015.1121944

Coleman, G. (2014). *Hacker, Hoaxer, Whistleblower, Spy: The Many Faces Of Anonymous*. London: Verso.

Csikszentmihalyi, M. (1990). *Flow: The psychology of optimal experience*. New York: Harper & Row.

Dahan, M. (2013). Hacking for the homeland: Patriotic hackers versus hacktivists. International Conference on Information Warfare and Security; Reading: Academic Conferences International Limited, 51–57.

Darley, J. M. (1992). Social organization for the production of evil. *Psychological Inquiry, 3*(2), 199–218. doi:10.1207/s15327965pli0302_28

Décary-Hétu, D., & Dupont, B. (2012). The social network of hackers. *Global Crime, 13*(3), 160–175. doi:10.1080/17440572.2012.702523

Deutsch, M., & Gerard, H. B. (1955). A study of normative and informational social influence upon individual judgment. *Journal of Abnormal Social Psychology, 51*, 629–636.

Dobusch, L., & Schoeneborn, D. (2015). Fluidity, identity, and organizationality: The communicative constitution of anonymous. *Journal of Management Studies, 52*(8), 1005–1035. doi:10.1111/joms.12139

Doise, W. (1978). *Groups and Individuals: Explanations in Social Psychology*. Cambridge: Cambridge University Press.

Donalds, C. M., & Osei-Bryson, K.-M. A. (2014). *A Cybercrime Taxonomy: Case of the Jamaican Jurisdiction*. Paper presented at the International Conference on Information Resources Management.

Dress, B. (2022). Why anti-trans web forum Kiwi Farms was erased from the internet. Retrieved from https://thehill.com/policy/technology/3642685-why-anti-trans-web-forum-kiwi-farms-was-erased-from-the-internet/

Dupont, B., Côté, A.-M., Boutin, J.-I., & Fernandez, J. (2017). Darkode: Recruitment Patterns and Transactional Features of "the Most Dangerous Cybercrime Forum in the World". *American Behavioral Scientist, 61*(11), 1219–1243. doi:10.1177/0002764217734263

Dupont, B., & Lusthaus, J. (2022). Countering Distrust in Illicit Online Networks: The Dispute Resolution Strategies of Cybercriminals. *Social Science Computer Review, 40*(4), 892–913. doi:10.1177/0894439321994623

Goffman, E. (1959). *The Presentation of Self in Everyday Life*. New York: Anchor Books.

Goode, S., & Cruise, S. (2006). What Motivates Software Crackers? *Journal of Business Ethics, 65*(2), 173–201. doi:10.1007/s10551-005-4709-9

Hald, S. L. N., & Pedersen, J. M. (2012, 19–22 Feb. 2012). *An updated taxonomy for characterizing hackers according to their threat properties.* Paper presented at the 2012 14th International Conference on Advanced Communication Technology (ICACT).

Hewstone, M., & Jaspars, J. M. F. (1982). Intergroup relations and attribution processes. In H. Tajfel (Ed.), *Social Identity And Intergroup Relations* (pp. 99–133). Cambridge: Cambridge University Press.

Holt, K. (2022). Kiwi Farms says someone hacked its website. Retrieved from https://tinyurl.com/bddfnknz

Holt, T., Freilich, J., & Chermak, S. (2017). Exploring the Subculture of Ideologically Motivated Cyber-Attackers. *Journal of Contemporary Criminal Justice, 33,* 104398621769910. doi:10.1177/1043986217699100

Holt, T., Kilger, M., Chiang, L., & Yang, C.-S. (2016). Exploring the Correlates of Individual Willingness to Engage in Ideologically Motivated Cyberattacks. *Deviant Behavior, 38,* 1–18. doi:10.1080/01639625.2016.1197008

Holt, T. J. (2007). Subcultural evolution? Examining the influence of on- and off-line experiences on deviant subcultures. *Deviant Behavior, 28*(2), 171–198. doi:10.1080/01639620601131065

Holt, T. J., & Bossler, A. M. (2014). An Assessment of the Current State of Cybercrime Scholarship. *Deviant Behavior, 35*(1), 20–40. doi:10.1080/01639625.2013.822209

Holt, T. J., Burruss, G. W., & Bossler, A. M. (2010). Social learning and cyber-deviance: examining the importance of a full social learning model in the virtual world. *Journal of Crime and Justice, 33*(2), 31–61. doi:10.1080/0735648X.2010.9721287

Holt, T. J., Freilich, J. D., & Chermak, S. M. (2017). Internet-based radicalization as enculturation to violent deviant subcultures. *Deviant Behavior, 38*(8), 855–869. doi:10.1080/0163962 5.2016.1197704

Holt, T. J., Kilger, M., Chiang, L., & Yang, C. (2015). Exploring the behavioral and attitudinal correlates of civilian cyberattacks. In M. Bouchard (Ed.), *Social networks, terrorism, and counter-terrorism: Radical and connected* (pp. 128–151). London: Routledge.

Holt, T. J., Smirnova, O., Chua, Y. T., & Copes, H. (2015). Examining the risk reduction strategies of actors in online criminal markets. *Global Crime, 16*(2), 81–103. doi:10.1080/17440 572.2015.1013211

Hughes, K. (1994). Entering the World-Wide Web. *ACM SIGWEB Newsletter, 3*(1), 4–8.

Hutchings, A. (2013). *Hacking and Fraud: Qualitative Analysis of Online Offending and Victimization.*

Hutchings, A., & Clayton, R. (2016). Exploring the Provision of Online Booter Services. *Deviant Behavior, 37*(10), 1163–1178. doi:10.1080/01639625.2016.1169829

Jaki, S., De Smedt, T., Gwozdz, M., Panchal, R., Rossa, A., & De Pauw, G. (2019). Online hatred of women in the Incels.me forum Linguistic analysis and automatic detection. *Journal of Language Aggression and Conflict, 7*(2), 240–268. doi:10.1075/jlac.00026

Jones, D. A., & Carroll, S. A. (2007). *Revenge is a dish best served cold: Avengers' accounts of calculated revenge cognitions and assessment of a proposed measure.* Paper presented at the IACM 2007 Meetings.

Kelman, H. C. (2006). Interests, relationships, identities: Three central issues for individuals and groups in negotiating their social environment. *Annual Review of Psychology, 57,* 1–26. doi:DOI 10.1146/annurev.psych.57.102904.190156

Kharpal, A., & Browne, R. (2021). Hackers return nearly half of the $600 million they stole in one of the biggest crypto heists. Retrieved from https://www.cnbc.com/2021/08/11/cryptocurrency-theft-hackers-steal-600-million-in-poly-network-hack.html

Kirwan, G., & Power, A. (2013). *Cybercrime: The Psychology of Online Offenders.* New York: Cambridge University Press.

Knappenberger, B. (Writer & Director). (2012). *We Are Legion: The Story of the Hacktivists.* Netflix.

Leukfeldt, E., Kleemans, E. R., & Stol, W. (2017). The Use of Online Crime Markets by Cybercriminal Networks: A View From Within. *American Behavioral Scientist, 61.* doi:10.1177/0002764217734267

Levell, J. (2022). *Boys, Childhood Domestic Abuse and Gang Involvement: Violence at Home, Violence On-Road.* Bristol: Bristol University Press.

Lu, Y., Luo, X., Polgar, M., & Cao, Y. (2010). Social Network Analysis of a Criminal Hacker Community. *Journal of Computer Information Systems, 51*(2), 31–41. doi:10.1080/08874417. 2010.11645466

Lusthaus, J. (2018). *Industry of anonymity: inside the business of cybercrime.* Cambridge, MA: Harvard University Press.

Lusthaus, J., Kleemans, E., Leukfeldt, R., Levi, M., & Holt, T. (2023). Cybercriminal networks in the UK and Beyond: Network structure, criminal cooperation and external interactions. *Trends in Organized Crime.* doi:10.1007/s12117-022-09476-9

Marques, J. M., Abrams, D., & Serodio, R. G. (2001). Being better by being right: Subjective group dynamics and derogation of in-group deviants when generic norms are undermined. *Journal of Personality and Social Psychology, 81*(3), 436–447. doi:10.1037/0022-3514.81.3.436

McAlaney, J., Bewick, B., & Hughes, C. (2011). The international development of the 'Social Norms' approach to drug education and prevention. *Drugs: Education, Prevention, and Policy, 18*(2), 81–89. doi:10.3109/09687631003610977

McAlaney, J., Hambidge, S., Kimpton, E., & Thackray, H. (2020, 7–11 Sept. 2020). *Knowledge is power: An analysis of discussions on hacking forums.* Paper presented at the 2020 IEEE European Symposium on Security and Privacy Workshops (EuroS&PW).

Milan, S. (2015). Hacktivism as a radical media practice. In Atton, C. (Ed.), *The Routledge companion to alternative and community media.* London: Routledge.

Moore, A. (1982–1989). *V for Vendetta.* London: Vertigo.

Murer, J., & Schwarze, T. (2022). Social Rituals of Pain: The Socio-Symbolic Meaning of Violence in Gang Initiations. *International Journal of Politics, Culture, and Society, 35*, 1–16. doi:10.1007/s10767-020-09392-2

NCA. (2016). NCA strategic cyber industry group cyber crime assessment 2016. In: NCA Rep., Natl. Crime Agency Strateg. Cyber Ind. Group London.

Nurse, J. R. C., & Bada, M. (2019). The Group Element of Cybercrime: Types, Dynamics, and Criminal Operations. In Attrill-Smith, A., Fulwood, C., Keep, M., & Kuss, D. J. (Eds), *The Oxford Handbook of Cyberpsychology.* Oxford: Oxford University Publishing.

Nykodym, N., Taylor, R., & Vilela, J. (2005). Criminal profiling and insider cyber crime. *Digital Investigation, 2*(4), 261–267. doi:10.1016/j.diin.2005.11.004

Olson, P. (2012). *We Are Anonymous.* New York: Back Bay Books.

Owen, T. (2015). *Disruptive Power: The Crisis of the State in the Digital Age.* Oxford: Oxford University Press.

Pastrana, S., Thomas, D., Hutchings, A., & Clayton, R. (2018). *CrimeBB: Enabling Cybercrime Research on Underground Forums at Scale.* Conference paper.

Pedersen, W. C., Bushman, B. J., Vasquez, E. A., & Miller, N. (2008). Kicking the (barking) dog effect: the moderating role of target attributes on triggered displaced aggression. *Pers Soc Psychol Bull, 34*(10), 1382–1395. doi:10.1177/0146167208321268

Perry, B., & Blazak, R. (2010). Places for races: The white supremacist movement imagines U.S. Geography. *Journal of Hate Studies, 8*, 29. doi:10.33972/jhs.67

Platt, C. (1994). Hackers: threat or menace? *Wired,* November 1994(2), 82–88.

Pless, M. (2016). Kiwi Farms, the Web's Biggest Community of Stalkers. *The New Yorker*, July 19.

Pratt, T., Cullen, F., Sellers, C., Winfree, J. L., Madensen, T., Daigle, L., . . . Gau, J. (2010). The Empirical Status of Social Learning Theory: A Meta-Analysis. *Justice Quarterly, 27*, 765–802. doi:10.1080/07418820903379610

Purtill, J. (2022). Hacker collective Anonymous declares 'cyber war' against Russia, disables state news website. Retrieved from https://www.abc.net.au/news/science/2022-02-25/hacker-collective-anonymous-declares-cyber-war-against-russia/100861160

Reicher, S. D., Spears, R., & Postmes, T. (1995). A social identity model of deindividuation phenomena. *European Review of Social Psychology, 6*(1), 161–198. doi:10.1080/1479277944300049

Rogers, M. (2010). The Psyche of Cybercriminals: A Psycho-Social Perspective. In Ghosh, S., and Turrini, E. (Eds), *Cybercrimes: A Multidisciplinary Analysis*. New York: Routledge, (pp. 217–235).

Schell, B. H., & Dodge, J. L. (2002). *The hacking of America: Who's doing it, why, and how*. Westport, CT: Greenwood Publishing Group Inc.

Seebruck, R. (2015). A typology of hackers: Classifying cyber malfeasance using a weighted arc circumplex model. *Digital Investigation, 14*, 36–45. doi:http://dx.doi.org/10.1016/j.diin.2015.07.002

Sherif, M., White, B. J., & Harvey, O. J. (1955). Status in experimentally produced groups. *American Journal of Sociology, 60*(4), 370–379. doi:10.1086/221569

Smith, E. R., Seger, C. R., & Mackie, D. A. (2007). Can emotions be truly group level? Evidence regarding four conceptual criteria. *Journal of Personality and Social Psychology, 93*(3), 431–446. doi:10.1037/0022-3514.93.3.431

Soudijn, M. R. J., & Zegers, B. C. H. T. (2012). Cybercrime and virtual offender convergence settings. *Trends in Organized Crime, 15*, 111–129.

Spears, R. (2021). Social Influence and Group Identity. In Fiske, S. T. (Ed.), *Annual Review of Psychology*, Vol. 72 (pp. 367–390).

Steinmetz, K. F. (2014). Craft(y)ness: An Ethnographic Study of Hacking. *The British Journal of Criminology, 55*(1), 125–145. doi:10.1093/bjc/azu061

Sugiura, L. (2021). *The incel rebellion: the rise of the manosphere and the virtual war against women* (First edition). Bingley, UK: Emerald Publishing Limited.

Suler, J. (2004). The online disinhibition effect. *Cyberpsychology & Behaviour, 7*(3), 321–326. doi:10.1089/1094931041291295

Tanis, M., & Postmes, T. (2005). A social identity approach to trust: interpersonal perception, group membership and trusting behaviour. *European Journal of Social Psychology, 35*(3), 413–424. doi:10.1002/ejsp.256

Tassev, L. (2022). Police in Kazakhstan Arrest Gang Forcing IT Specialists to Run Crypto Farms. Retrieved from https://news.bitcoin.com/police-in-kazakhstan-arrest-gang-forcing-it-specialists-to-run-crypto-farms/

Thackray, H. (2019). *Hackers gonna hack: Investigating the effect of group processes and social identities within online hacking communities*. PhD, Bournemouth University, Poole.

Thackray, H., & McAlaney, J. (2018). Groups Online: Hacktivism and Social Protest. In J. McAlaney, L. A. Frumkin, & V. Benson (Eds), *Psychologicaland Behavioral Examinations in Cyber Security*. Hershey, PA: IGI Global.

Thackray, H., Richardson, C., Dogan, H., Taylor, J., & McAlaney, J. (2017). *Surveying the hackers: The challenges of data collection from a secluded community*. Paper presented at the 16th European Conference on Cyber Warfare and Security, Dublin.

Troia, V. (2020). *Hunting Cyber Criminals: A Hacker's Guide to Online Intelligence Gathering Tools and Techniques*. Indianapolis, IN: Wiley.

Veale, K. (2020). Gaming the Rules. In *Gaming the Dynamics of Online Harassment* (pp. 87–106). Cham: Springer International Publishing.

Wallach, M. A., Kogan, N., & Bem, D. J. (1962). Group influence on individual risk-taking. *Journal of Abnormal Psychology, 65*(2), 75–86. doi:10.1037/H0044376

Williams, M. L., Levi, M., Burnap, P., & Gundur, R. V. (2019). Under the corporate radar: Examining insider business cybercrime victimization through an application of Routine Activities Theory. *Deviant Behavior, 40*(9), 1119–1131. doi:10.1080/01639625.2018.1461786

Woo, H. J. (2003). *The hacker mentality: exploring the relationship between psychological variables and hacking activities*. PhD, University of Georgia.

Wood, W., Lundgren, S., Ouellette, J. A., Busceme, S., & Blackstone, T. (1994). Minority influence: a meta-analytic review of social influence processes. *Psychological Bulletin, 115*(3), 323–345. doi:10.1037/0033-2909.115.3.323

Yip, M., Webber, C., & Shadbolt, N. (2013). Trust among cybercriminals? Carding forums, uncertainty and implications for policing. *Policing and Society, 23*(4), 516–539. doi:10.1080/10439463.2013.780227

Victimology and resilience **4**

Context

Cybersecurity breaches may often be seen as being technical in nature, however they invariably impact on people. The most obvious example is when an individual loses money through some type of breach of their bank accounts. However other forms of cyber victimisation exist. For example, an employee who unwittingly facilitates a cyber breach at an organisation during a social engineering attack may feel shame and guilt at their role in the breach. As will be discussed further in Chapter 6 they may also be penalised by their organisation for their part in the attack. Even if no blame is placed on any individuals, employees in the organisation may feel increased anxiety and vulnerability over there having been a breach. More broadly, cyber breaches of organisations and systems can undermine public trust in socio-technical systems, including online shopping, potentially effecting future sales, or electronic voting, impacting future engagement. As such there can be multiple societal impacts of cybercrime that extend beyond the immediate harms to the targeted victims. Nevertheless, there remains relatively little research on victimology in cybercrime compared to traditional forms of crime (Halder, 2022). It has been argued that women and children can be considered the most vulnerable victims in cybercrime. This includes women from lower socio-economic backgrounds who are targeted by porn content dealers, a form of abuse that continues to impact the victim indefinitely beyond the creation of the materials. This impacts not only the individual victim, but also their friends and family (Halder, 2022).

The role of employees in cyber breaches can broadly be separated into unintentional and intentional insider threat. Unintentional insider threat is when

DOI: 10.4324/9781003300359-4

an individual such as an employee clicks on a malicious link within a phishing email without realising that they are exposing the organisation to risk. Similarly, an employee who unwillingly facilitates a social engineering attack by giving a social engineer information about the current waste collection services used by a company could be considered an insider threat. Simple cases of human error can also potentially create insider threats, such as with the incident of a Japanese employee of a financial company who, following a night of heavy drinking, lost a USB stick with the residents of the city of Amagasaki's personal details on it (BBC News, 2022). One of the challenges in preventing unintentional insider threat is often the scale of the issue. As noted previously, it only takes one employee in a company to have a moment of intention and click on a phishing link for an attack to potentially be successful. Intentional insider threat on the other hand refers to when an individual deliberately takes action that causes harm to the organisation. This includes acts of revenge or industrial espionage of the type discussed in Chapter 2. The CERT National Insider Threat Center provides detailed definitions of these two types of insider threat:

> [An insider threat is] a current or former employee, contractor, or business partner who has or had authorized access to an organization's network, system, or data and has intentionally exceeded or intentionally used that access in a manner that negatively affected the confidentiality, integrity, availability, or physical well-being of the organization's information, information systems, or workforce. [An unintentional insider is] a current or former employee, contractor, or other business partner who has or had authorized access to an organization's network, system, or data and who, through their action/inaction without malicious intent causes harm or substantially increases the probability of future serious harm to the confidentiality, integrity, or availability of the organization's information or information systems. (Brackney & Anderson, 2004)

The risk and harms caused by insider threat can be worsened by a lack of detection, slow response, and inconsistent remediation policies (Ko, Divakaran, Liau, & Thing, 2017). Despite this, it has been argued that insider threats are an under-estimated and under-addressed cybersecurity threat to organisations (Ponemon Institute, 2020). Concern about this risk is also reported to have increased during the COVID-19 pandemic, due to the rise of remote working (Tessian, 2020). The United Nations reported a 600% increase in malicious emails during the pandemic (Lederer, 2020). Kemp, Buil-Gil, Moneva, Miro-Llinares, and Diaz-Castano (2021) observe however that the relationship between reductions in offline crime and increases in online crime during the pandemic were complex and nuanced. For example, it has been observed that cyber-attacks that occurred during the height of the pandemic may have been undetected and unreported as businesses dealt with daily challenges (Department for Digital, Culture, Media and Sport, 2021).

As noted by Bossler and Holt (2013) it is difficult to get a sense of the scale of cyber victimisation due to several issues. Firstly, victims may not realise that they are victims. For example, the exact means by which a successful social engineering attack was conducted may be something that a company is unable to ever establish, assuming that they are even aware that an attack has taken place. Secondly, those who are aware they have been victimised may not report the incident and might not believe the authorities will do anything, or think that they will be judged negatively for having fallen for a scam or being caught out by a phishing email. It has been suggested that men are likely to disengage with the criminal justice system if they perceive they are experiencing victim blaming following a cyber-attack, and that women will often not report the crime at all, due to concerns of victim blaming (Halder, 2022). This may be a valid concern for individuals to have – it has been observed that there is often a view by the authorities that victims of online fraud have themselves to blame (Villiers, 2009).

Risk factors

There has been research into why people are tricked by social engineering attacks, with most work focussing on characteristics and individual differences that predict how people react to phishing emails. Early work in this field demonstrated that individuals often do not look at key indicators of the legitimacy of a website, such as the address bar (Dhamija, Tygar, & Hearst, 2006). In a study of 382 participants, Dhamija et al. (2006) found a phishing rate detection rate of 65.63%, with only six participants achieving a 100% detection rate. There was a statistically significant correlation between participants' confidence in their ability to detect a phishing email and their success rate at doing so, although many of those who were highly confident in their own abilities were still fooled. Research has also found that there are factors which are predictive of cybersecurity behaviours that would not perhaps occur to cybersecurity practitioners to take into consideration, such as religious beliefs (Kelecha & Belanger, 2013). This reflects the fundamental challenge involved in assessing how much at risk an individual is at being a victim of cybercrime – humans are complex and predicting who will be a victim is no less challenging than predicting how an individual will behave in any given situation.

A further challenge in preventing people from becoming a victim of cybercrime is that digital technologies provide services and opportunities with an ease that is not always available offline, or even available at all. The benefits that these technologies bring could lead people to continue using them, even if they are aware they are at risk. It has been found for instance that people do not tend to alter their use of social network sites even if they have been hacked (O'Connell & Kirwan, 2014). This could reflect a conflict between the motivation to protect oneself and the motivation to impression manage. Impression management was first described in 1959 (Goffman, 1959) and states that we aim to influence others to see us in our desired way. It has been studied extensively in psychological research (Bolino, Long, & Turnley, 2016), and as discussed in Chapter 3 is something that is heavily exploited by social engineers. This need to shape how one is seen by the world through the sharing of information, and the desire to protect oneself from intrusion, is known as the privacy paradox (Utz & Kramer, 2009). As technology becomes increasingly inter-connected and greater use is made of social media platforms it seems inevitable that people will feel pressured to manage how their identity is seen online, which in turn provides attackers with information that can be used as the basis for an attack. The permanency of information posted online can also be a factor – for example a post made by someone in their youth could potentially be used against them later in life when they are in a senior or sensitive position. It is interesting to note that companies now exist that an individual can pay to review and, if necessary, remove internet posts that individual has made over their life and which could be considered offensive.

Research into demographics of cyber victimology has produced conflicting results. For example, studies have found both younger and older people to be at greatest risk (Sheng et al., 2010), with inconsistent and contradictory results found in other research studies (Maimon & Louderback, 2019), including in relation to phishing emails (Lichtenberg, Sugarman, Paulson, Ficker, & Rahman-Filipiak, 2016). In contrast, Reyns (2013) identified those most at risk in the UK to be male, elderly or in one of the higher socio-economic groups. Lin et al. (2019) explored why older adults appear to be more i) targeted by and ii) vulnerable to phishing emails. They note that older people are the fastest growing demographic group in many countries, such as the USA; they have accumulated wealth; and they are more likely to be in positions of power and influence. This latter point relates to spear-phishing, in which senior members of a company are specifically targeted by social engineers and hackers, on the basis that such individuals have the most access to company systems. As such, the apparent increased rate of victimisation of older adults may at least in part be an artefact of them being at a disproportionate risk of being targeted by cyber-attackers. Cognitive processing in older adults may be reduced, although it is important to stress that there is a distinction between normal changes in cognitive processes with age and the development of medical conditions such as Alzheimer's disease. In addition, older adults are naturally less likely to have had experience of computers in their youth.

There is less research on the role of other risk factors. Lin et al. (2019) did not for example find any relationship between race or ethnicity and likelihood of victimisation. It has been found that people who exhibit low self-control are more likely to have their password compromised, but are not at any different risk for other types of attack (Maimon & Louderback, 2019). Cognitive decision-making style also appeared to be related to likelihood of victimisation. Jones, Towse, Race, and Harrison (2019) argue that differences in working memory – conceptualised by some researchers as being similar to short term memory – may be one reason why some people will employ heuristics when reading a phishing email whilst others may not. Jones et al. (2019) further note that in contrast to previous research they found no evidence that either personality traits or self-control have any influence on susceptibility. However, Kleitman, Law, and Kay (2018) have reported some evidence of personality being a risk factor, with for example openness being positively associated with susceptibility to phishing emails in some studies, but negatively associated in other studies. In their study Kleitman et al. (2018) found that people whose first language is English were more likely to spot English language mistakes in phishing emails, which is perhaps not surprising. This highlights a risk inherent in English being the de facto language used for international business transactions in many parts of the world. Kleitman et al. (2018) also note a significant but weak positive correlation between self-reported ability to spot phishing emails and actual ability. Coupled with the heuristics and biases discussed previously, this could lead people to be overconfident about their ability to reduce their risk of cyber victimisation. This overconfidence is of course something that is often actively exploited by social engineers and other attackers.

Lin et al. (2019) suggest that one of the reasons behind the inconsistent results in risk factor research is the use of self-report in previous studies, as this may not be a reliable methodological approach with which to collect data in some contexts. They also report a discrepancy between people's perceived and actual susceptibility to phishing emails, a gap that was more pronounced in older adults. A related methodological issue is that individuals may misperceive their own abilities, as well as how much risk they are at. Rifon, LaRose, and Choi (2005) noted that users were more likely to ignore warnings about potential dangers if they deemed themselves to be effective at minimising the effects of privacy breaches. This is a challenge, as it has also been found that people tend to perceive themselves to be at less risk than their peers (Schmidt & Arnett, 2005). Nieto and Rios (2019) argue that the data generated in cybercrime can be used to generate profiles of victims, as part of Human Factors Cybersecurity (HFC). However, one of the fundamental challenges in identifying risk factors for being a victim of cybercrime is that this requires complete and full knowledge of the activities that a person engages in, and how objectively risky these activities are.

Cybercriminals do of course often actively seek to hide the fact that they are trying to attack a victim and, often in the case of social engineering, ideally wish that their crime is never detected at all. Nevertheless, it may be that risk factors can be more easily identified in organisational settings, where the organisation can more directly observe the behaviour of individuals. This can potentially be combined with analytical approaches used with big data, as will be discussed in more detail in Chapters 6 and 7.

Specific types of cybercrime appear to be associated with specific risk factors. Whitty (2018) examined the psychological characteristics of people who have been victims of romance scams. A romance scam involves the use of psychological manipulation to make the target believe that they are in a romantic relationship with the scammer. The scammer feigns an emotional relationship with the target, and then once this has been established begins to make requests for financial support, or access personal details such as social security credentials that can then be used for identity theft and fraud. This can involve the creation of fake dating profiles. The majority of victims were found to be middle aged, highly educated, and female, although as noted by Whitty (2018) there are some conflicts in the literature. The consequences of being a victim of romance scams are not just financial losses but also the emotional trauma caused by feelings of betrayal and humiliation. Similarly, it has also been noted that the victims of other types of cyber-attack such as online hate speech are more likely to be women, both those women with a public profile such as content creators or entrepreneurs (Halder, 2022) and women who are targeted by male supervisors and colleagues (Tenório Junior & Bjorn, 2019). This can be impacted by culture, with women from non-Western cultures being less likely to seek justice for being a victim of cybercrime compared to their Western counterparts, due to lack of awareness, fear of social taboos, and lack of digital empowerment (Halder & Jaishankar, 2012). In contrast, it has been suggested that men are more likely to be victims of sextortion, in which the victim is coerced into committing sexual acts on webcam and subsequently blackmailed with threats of release of this footage to friends, family, and colleagues (Aitken, Gaskell, & Hodkinson, 2018). Overall, Halder (2022) reports that women are more likely to experience several forms of cybercrime including interpersonal cybercrimes, dating scams, cyber sexual offences, data privacy infringement, reputational damage, and physical assault on the basis of cyberstalking. Conversely, men are more likely to experience cybercrimes that include lottery scams, e-commerce frauds, recruitment for terrorism purposes, online racial hatred and hate speech, and sextortion. In both cases, men and women aged over 50 may be at an increased risk of banking frauds (Halder, 2022).

Jeffries and Apeh (2020) note that there are several differences in investigating crime online as opposed to offline crimes. This is complicated by lack of standard operating procedures for investigation and training for police officers, along with a focus on child protection topics and less work on other forms of cybercrimes. The inclusion of civil resources may also be something that could be done to a greater extent, as proposed by Chung et al. (2006). It has been suggested that cybercrime prevention and investigation strategies are already being handled by agencies outside of government and law enforcement. Sikra, Renaud, and Thomas (2023) propose the term Responsibilised Non-Policing Agencies (RNPAs) to refer to such agencies, which are identified as commonly consisting of a mixture of charities and banks. These RNPAs place a buffer between the victims of cybercrimes and the state and police. As Sikra, Renaud, and Thomas (2023) observe there are both costs and opportunities associated with this role of RNPAs in cybercrime victimisation and reporting. RNPAs have more expertise available and greater experience of cybercrimes and may have lower costs than the police, but victims themselves prefer support from specialised police officers over RNPAs. Overall, they characterise the use of RNPAs as resulting in higher volumes of lower quality work getting done, and the use of specialised policing as resulting in lower volumes of higher quality work being done. As seems to be a recurrent theme throughout all aspects of cybersecurity, there is an unavoidable trade-off between efficiency and cost.

Overall, there are many challenges in reducing the risk that people face of becoming a victim of cyber-attack. Given the scope of cyber-attacks and the skill of attackers in targeting their victims, there is an argument that it is not in fact possible to completely remove all risk. The former CEO of Equifax, Richard Smith, faced criticism when testifying to Congress following a serious customer data breach at the company, with the comment that "I don't think we can pass a law that fixes stupid" (Rushe, 2017). Whilst it is not constructive to label people who have been a victim of a cyber-attack as lacking intelligence – keeping in mind that the victims of cybercrime have included senior staff at technology companies – there is a broader point that human error will always occur. As discussed in Chapter 2, the cognitive biases and heuristics that humans use to navigate our social world, and which social engineers seek to manipulate, have evolved to serve a purpose. As will be discussed further in Chapter 6, it is important that prevention and behaviour-change strategies that aim to reduce the risk of cyber victimisation take into consideration the underlying reasons for risk factors.

Resilience

If it is accepted that cyber-attacks are common, and that anyone can potentially become a victim, then the next step is considering how individuals and organisations can be resilient to these threats. Resilience has been defined in various ways in the research literature, but most definitions share the same basic conceptualisation of resilience as being a positive adaptation in the face of adversity (Sutcliffe & Vogus, 2003). Resilience has been considered at an individual level as a stable personality trait, a state-like developable capacity, or a process (Kossek & Perrigino, 2016). It is of note that these latter two conceptualisations suggest that resilience can be malleable, as opposed to a fixed trait, which is relevant to the topic of behaviour change, as will be discussed in Chapter 6. These differing concepts are reflected in the diversity of scales that have been developed to measure resilience (Hartmann, Weiss, Newman, & Hoegl, 2020). Similarly, Fisher, Ragsdale, and Fisher (2019) argue that resilience mechanisms can best be understood as those experiences, reactions, and behaviours that individuals apply in the face of adversity, such as certain coping strategies or emotional responses. In support of these arguments, several individual factors have been identified in the research literature that appear to be linked to resilience. These include conscientiousness and self-efficacy (Lyons, Schweitzer, & Ng, 2015), business confidence (Yang & Danes, 2014), locus of control (Stevenson, Phillips, & Anderson, 2011), reflective ability (Kinman & Grant, 2010), emotional intelligence (Förster & Duchek, 2017), and work related attitudes (Badran & Youssef-Morgan, 2015). Working in a military context, Lee, Sudom, and Zamorski (2013) noted that there appears to be complex relationships between psychological resilience and potential protective factors in Canadian military personnel, although conscientiousness, emotional stability, and positive social interactions appeared to be important.

Team resilience considers resilience as a collective phenomenon that is conceptually distinct from individual resilience (Carmeli, Friedman, & Tishler, 2013). As such it is something that would appear to be especially relevant to organisational culture and organisational-level behaviour change strategies, although it has been noted that, compared to individual resilience, the concept of team resilience is less developed (Bowers, Kreutzer, Cannon-Bowers, & Lamb, 2017). Hartmann et al. (2020) argued that predictors of team level resilience can be grouped in terms of emotions, interpersonal processes, and structural aspects of the group. They also note that a group consisting of individually resilient team members does not necessarily result in team resilience, which highlights the important of organisational culture and how the members of an organisation communicate and interact with one another. Although research specifically on team resilience is lacking, research on other collective-level constructs, such as collective efficacy or collective creativity, has demonstrated the importance of explicitly accounting for coordinative, relational, and interactive aspects of teams (Bandura, 2000).

It has been further argued that resilience should be considered in the context of the circumstances in which that resilience is being evoked. This could consist of isolated but high-intensity circumstances (for example a crisis such as a cyber-attack), or may consist of high-frequency, high-duration circumstances, such as ongoing work stress (Hartmann et al., 2020). This is consistent with research in the literature that suggests that the experience of resilience is specific to the domain and context in which it occurs, for example in the workplace or one's personal life (Todt, Weiss, & Hoegl, 2018). In an attempt to chart this diverse, interdisciplinary research literature, Linnenluecke identified five streams of research into organisational resilience, as based on bibliographic mapping of the literature (Linnenluecke, 2017):

- Organisational resilience in relation to crisis management, e.g., Williams, Gruber, Sutcliffe, Shepherd, and Zhao (2017)
- Occupation specific aspects of employee resilience, e.g., Kossek and Perrigino (2016)
- Differing conceptualisations of employee resilience and resilience building programmes, e.g., Britt, Shen, Sinclair, Grossman, and Klieger (2016)
- The development of resilience as a behavioural capability, e.g., Kuntz, Malinen, and Näswall (2017)
- The effectiveness of resilience-building programmes in organisations, e.g., Vanhove, Herian, Perez, Harms, and Lester (2016)

These five strands of research demonstrate the differing focuses and underlying positions of studies in this field. Firstly, there is difference between individual resilience vs organisational/ team-based resilience. Secondly, there is difference between resilience as an individual and fixed personality trait vs resilience as a malleable capacity. Finally, there is difference between resilience as a response to a crisis vs resilience as a long-term strategy. These differences create challenges in coming to a cohesive view on what resilience is, and how it should be applied to behaviour change and harm reduction in cybersecurity. Methodological limitations have also been identified within the literature. As Hartmann et al. (2020) state there is a lack of clear understanding on how the theories often cited in relation to organisational resilience underpin the process of developing resilience. As shall be discussed in Chapter 6 this has parallels with the research relating to behaviour change, where it has been observed that it is not always clear how theories of behaviour are being used to implement behaviour-change strategies. In addition, there are issues around the reliability and validity of the instruments that have been used to measure organisational resilience, which is in part due to the different ways resilience has been conceptualised.

There is relatively little research on resilience specifically in the content found to focus on cybersecurity contexts, with a handful of authors being responsible for most of the substantive work that has been undertaken. Cyber resilience is discussed in this literature as a technological process. For example, Petrenko (2019) proposes the following definition: "Cyber Resilience is an ability of the cyber-system functioning, according to a certain algorithm, in order to achieve the operational purpose under the intruder information and technical influences". Petrenko (2019) states that resilience in cyber systems can further be considered in terms of active and passive resilience. Active resilience is composed of factors such as reliability, response and recovery, and survivability. It is inherent in complex systems where behaviours are based on a decision to act. That is, there is a preferred state of the system which is achieved through purposeful behaviour. Passive resilience on the other hand is composed of factors such as strength, balance, and homeostasis. It is inherent in a simple system, where there is no decision act involved. It could be argued that the fewer decisions required the less of an opportunity there is for social engineers and attackers to manipulate decision making processes to their advantage. However, businesses often must change their practices to adapt to societal and financial demands, as well as changes in technology. As such, an organisation that seeks to be resilient to the impact of cyber-attacks has to consider this as being a long-term requirement that requires continual review and revision.

Wood and Hollnagel (2006) put forward an engineering-based view of resilience that is relevant to the cyber context and is based upon four factors that are intrinsic to the system that users are engaging with:

1. Ability to learn: learn from past events (factual), understand what happened and why;
2. Ability to respond: respond to actual (regular and irregular conditions) in an effective, flexible manner;
3. Ability to monitor: monitor short-term developments and threats (critical), as well as revise risk models; and
4. Ability to anticipate: anticipate long-term threats and opportunities (potential).

This conceptualisation does acknowledge the human factors in resilience through a recognition of the importance of the ability to learn from past events, but nevertheless the conceptualisation is focussed on resilience primarily on technical and systems issues. This is consistent with one of the few studies on cybersecurity resilience in a military setting, namely a NATO funded study on cybersecurity resilience in the Arctic (Trump, Hossain, & Linkov, 2020). In that case the role of human factors was again acknowledged, but not seen as a resource to be built upon. This is consistent with observations that have been made that cybersecurity research often treats humans as the problem rather than being part of a potential solution to cybersecurity challenges (Zimmermann & Renaud, 2019). Aoyama, Naruoka, Koshijima, Machii, and Seki (2015a) mapped cyber resilience factors, common security activities, and broader resilience factors. Cyber resilience factors were grouped into prevention, detection, and response. Common security activities and corresponding resilience factors are identified under each of these cyber resilience factors. For example, security activities under prevention include threat analysis and attack forecast, with the appropriate resilience factor being to anticipate. Detection cyber resilience security activities include monitoring and intrusion detection, which come under the resilience factor of monitoring. Finally, cyber resilience related to response includes security activities such as incident reports and impact analysis, with regard to the two resilience factors of responding and learning. This point of learning from a cybersecurity incident is something that ethical social engineers also stress is an extremely important process for organisations to engage with, although they also note that this does not always seem to happen (Radcliffe, 2023). In constructing this mapping, Aoyama, Naruoka, Koshijima, Machii, and Seki (2015b) also note that research into the human contribution of cyber resilience is limited, which they propose is due to the difficulties in observing organisations' responses to actual cyber-attacks. As they comment, training exercises are instead used to explore cyber resilience. However, despite this greater focus on human factors, the classification they propose of cyber resilience is still based primarily on technical and systems aspects.

Overall, the literature on the conceptualisation of resilience could be split into research that considers resilience as an individual, psychological construct, and research that considers resilience in terms of the system in which humans operate, with a focus on technological elements. Not surprisingly, research that uses the former conceptualisation comes from social sciences disciplines, whereas the latter conceptualisations are more evident in computing and IT sources. The research specifically on cybersecurity resilience is a small sub-set of the wider research on organisational resilience and is based primarily on the more technology and systems focussed conceptualisations of resilience. Aspects of how to increase resilience of both types will be discussed in further detail in Chapter 6.

References

Aitken, S., Gaskell, D., & Hodkinson, A. (2018). Online Sexual Grooming: Exploratory Comparison of Themes Arising From Male Offenders' Communications with Male Victims Compared to Female Victims. *Deviant Behavior, 39*(9), 1170–1190. doi:10.1080/01639625. 2017.1410372

Aoyama, T., Naruoka, H., Koshijima, I., Machii, W., & Seki, K. (2015a). *Studying resilient cyber incident management from large-scale cyber security training.* Paper presented at the 2015 10th Asian Control Conference: Emerging Control Techniques for a Sustainable World, ASCC 2015.

Aoyama, T., Naruoka, H., Koshijima, I., Machii, W., & Seki, K. (2015b). *Studying resilient cyber incident management from large-scale cyber security training.* Paper presented at the 10th Asian Control Conference (ASCC), Kota Kinabalu, MALAYSIA, May 31–Jun 03.

Badran, M. A. R., & Youssef-Morgan, C. M. (2015). Psychological capital and job satisfaction in Egypt. *Journal of Managerial Psychology, 30,* 354–370.

Bandura, A. (2000). Exercise of human agency through collective efficacy. *Current Directions in Psychological Science, 9*(3), 75–78. doi:10.1111/1467–8721.00064

BBC News. (2022). Japanese man loses USB stick with entire city's personal details. Retrieved from https://www.bbc.co.uk/news/world-asia-61921222

Bolino, M., Long, D., & Turnley, W. (2016). Impression Management in Organizations: Critical Questions, Answers, and Areas for Future Research. In Morgeson, F. P. (Ed.), *Annual Review of Organizational Psychology and Organizational Behavior, Vol. 3* (pp. 377–406).

Bossler, A. M., & Holt, T. J. (2013). Assessing officer perceptions and support for online community policing. *Security Journal, 26*(4), 349–366. doi:10.1057/sj.2013.23

Bowers, C., Kreutzer, C., Cannon-Bowers, J., & Lamb, J. (2017). Team resilience as a second-order emergent state: A theoretical model and research directions. *Frontiers in Psychology, 8.* doi:10.3389/fpsyg.2017.01360

Brackney, R. C., & Anderson, R. H. (2004). *Understanding the insider threat. Proceedings of a March 2004 workshop.* Retrieved from https://www.rand.org/content/dam/rand/pubs/conf_proceedings/2005/RAND_CF196.pdf

Britt, T. W., Shen, W., Sinclair, R. R., Grossman, M. R., & Klieger, D. M. (2016). How much do we really know about employee resilience? *Industrial and Organizational Psychology, 9*(2), 378–404. doi:10.1017/iop.2015.107

Carmeli, A., Friedman, Y., & Tishler, A. (2013). Cultivating a resilient top management team: The importance of relational connections and strategic decision comprehensiveness. *Safety Science, 51*(1), 148–159. doi:10.1016/j.ssci.2012.06.002

Chung, W., Chen, H.-c., Chang, W., & Chou, S. (2006). Fighting cybercrime: A review and the Taiwan experience. *Decision Support Systems, 41,* 669–682. doi:10.1016/j.dss.2004.06.006

Department for Digital, Culture, Media, and Sport. (2021). Cyber Security Breaches Survey 2021. Retrieved from https://assets.publishing.service.gov.uk/government/uploads/system/uploads/attachment_data/file/972399/Cyber_Security_Breaches_Survey_2021_Statistical_Release.pdf

Dhamija, R., Tygar, J., & Hearst, M. (2006). *Why phishing works (Vol. 1).* Proceedings of the SIGCHI Conference on Human Factors in Computing Systems.

Fisher, D. M., Ragsdale, J. M., & Fisher, E. C. S. (2019). The importance of definitional and temporal issues in the study of resilience. *Applied Psychology: An International Review, 68*(4), 583–620. doi:10.1111/apps.12162

Förster, C., & Duchek, S. (2017). What makes leaders resilient? An exploratory interview study. *German Journal of Human Resource Management, 31*(4), 281–306. doi:10.1177/2397002217709400

Goffman, E. (1959). *The Presentation of Self in Everyday Life.* New York: Anchor Books.

Halder, D. (2022). *Cyber victimology: decoding cyber crime victimization.* New York: Routledge.

Halder, D., & Jaishankar, K. (2012). *Cyber crime and the victimization of women: laws, rights and regulations.* Hershey, PA: Information Science Reference.

Hartmann, S., Weiss, M., Newman, A., & Hoegl, M. (2020). Resilience in the workplace: A multilevel review and synthesis. *Applied Psychology, 69*(3), 913–959. doi:https://doi.org/10.1111/apps.12191

Jeffries, S., & Apeh, E. (2020). Standard operating procedures for cybercrime investigations: a systematic literature review. In Benson, V. & McAlaney, J. (Eds), *Emerging Cyber Threats and Cognitive Vulnerabilities* (pp. 145–162). London: Academic Press.

Jones, H. S., Towse, J. N., Race, N., & Harrison, T. (2019). Email fraud: The search for psychological predictors of susceptibility. *PLoS One, 14*(1), e0209684–e0209684. doi:10.1371/journal.pone.0209684

Kelecha, B. B., & Belanger, F. (2013). *Religiosity and information security policy compliance.* Paper presented at the Americas conference on information systems, Chicago, IL, 15–17 August.

Kemp, S., Buil-Gil, D., Moneva, A., Miro-Llinares, F., & Diaz-Castano, N. (2021). Empty Streets, Busy Internet: A Time-Series Analysis of Cybercrime and Fraud Trends During COVID-19. *Journal of Contemporary Criminal Justice, 37*(4), 480–501. doi:10.1177/10439862211027986

Kinman, G., & Grant, L. (2010). Exploring stress resilience in trainee social workers: The role of emotional and social competencies. *The British Journal of Social Work, 41*(2), 261–275. doi:10.1093/bjsw/bcq088

Kleitman, S., Law, M. K. H., & Kay, J. (2018). It's the deceiver and the receiver: Individual differences in phishing susceptibility and false positives with item profiling. *PLoS One, 13*(10), e0205089-e0205089. doi:10.1371/journal.pone.0205089

Ko, L. L., Divakaran, D. M., Liau, Y. S., & Thing, V. L. L. (2017). Insider threat detection and its future directions. *Int. J. Secur. Netw., 12*(3), 168–187. doi:10.1504/ijsn.2017.084391

Kossek, E. E., & Perrigino, M. B. (2016). Resilience: A Review Using a Grounded Integrated Occupational Approach. *The Academy of Management Annals, 10*(1), 729–797. doi:10.1080/19416520.2016.1159878

Kuntz, J. R. C., Malinen, S., & Näswall, K. (2017). Employee resilience: Directions for resilience development. *Consulting Psychology Journal: Practice and Research, 69*(3), 223–242. doi:10.1037/cpb0000097

Lederer, E. M. (2020). Top UN official warns malicious emails on rise in pandemic. Retrieved from https://apnews.com/general-news-c7e7fc7e582351f8f55293d0bf21d7fb

Lee, J. E. C., Sudom, K. A., & Zamorski, M. A. (2013). Longitudinal analysis of psychological resilience and mental health in Canadian military personnel returning from overseas deployment. *Journal of Occupational Health Psychology, 18*(3), 327–337. Retrieved from https://eurekamag.com/research/054/174/054174438.php

Lichtenberg, P. A., Sugarman, M. A., Paulson, D., Ficker, L. J., & Rahman-Filipiak, A. (2016). Psychological and functional vulnerability predicts fraud cases in older adults: Results of a longitudinal study. *Clinical Gerontologist, 39*(1), 48–63. doi:10.1080/07317115.2015.1101632

Lin, T., Capecci, D. E., Ellis, D. M., Rocha, H. A., Dommaraju, S., Oliveira, D. S., & Ebner, N. C. (2019). Susceptibility to spear-phishing emails: Effects of internet user demographics and email content. *ACM Transactions on Computer-Human Interaction, 26*(5), 28. doi:10.1145/3336141

Linnenluecke, M. K. (2017). Resilience in Business and Management Research: A Review of Influential Publications and a Research Agenda. *International Journal of Management Reviews, 19*(1), 4–30. doi:https://doi.org/10.1111/ijmr.12076

Lyons, S. T., Schweitzer, L., & Ng, E. S. W. (2015). Resilience in the modern career. *Career Development International, 20*(4), 363–383. doi:10.1108/CDI-02-2015-0024

Maimon, D., & Louderback, E. R. (2019). Cyber-dependent crimes: An interdisciplinary review. *Annual Review of Criminology, 2*(1), 191–216. doi:10.1146/annurev-criminol-032317-092057

Nieto, A., & Rios, R. (2019). Cybersecurity profiles based on human-centric IoT devices. *Human-centric Computing and Information Sciences, 9*(1), 39. doi:10.1186/s13673-019-0200-y

O'Connell, R., & Kirwan, G. (2014). Protection Motivation Theory and online activities. In Power, A. & Kirwan, G. (Eds), *Cyberpsychology and New Media: A Thematic Reader.* New York: Psychology Press.

Petrenko, S. (2019). *Cyber Resilience.* Aalborg: River Publishers.

Ponemon Institute. (2020). *2020 cost of insider threats: global report*. Retrieved from https://www.exclusive-networks.com/uk/wp-content/uploads/sites/28/2020/12/UK-VR-Proofpoint-Report-2020-Cost-of-Insider-Threats.pdf

Radcliffe, J. (2023). *People Hacker: Confessions of a Burglar for Hire*. London: Simon & Schuster.

Reyns, B. W. (2013). Online Routines and Identity Theft Victimization: Further Expanding Routine Activity Theory beyond Direct-Contact Offenses. *Journal of Research in Crime and Delinquency, 50*(2), 216–238. doi:10.1177/0022427811425539

Rifon, N. J., LaRose, R., & Choi, S. M. (2005). Your privacy is sealed: Effects of web privacy seals on trust and personal disclosures. *Journal of Consumer Affairs, 39*(2), 339–362. doi:10.1111/j.1745–6606.2005.00018.x

Rushe, D. (2017). 'No law can fix stupid': Congress slams former Equifax CEO for data hack. Retrieved from https://www.theguardian.com/business/2017/oct/03/former-equifax-ceo-deeply-regrets-how-company-handled-data-hack

Schmidt, M. B., & Arnett, K. P. (2005). Spyware: A little knowledge is a wonderful thing. *Communications of the ACM, 48*(8), 67–70. doi:10.1145/1076211.1076242

Sheng, S., Holbrook, M., Kumaraguru, P., Cranor, L., Downs, J., & ACM. (2010). *Who Falls for Phish? A Demographic Analysis of Phishing Susceptibility and Effectiveness of Interventions.* New York: Assoc Computing Machinery.

Sikra, J., Renaud, K. V., & Thomas, D. R. (2023). UK Cybercrime Victims and Reporting: A Systematic Review. *Commonwealth Cybercrime Journal, 1*(1), 28–59.

Stevenson, A. D., Phillips, C. B., & Anderson, K. (2011). Resilience among doctors who work in challenging areas: a qualitative study. *The British journal of general practice: the journal of the Royal College of General Practitioners, 61* 588, e404–410.

Sutcliffe, K. M., & Vogus, T. J. (2003). *Organizing For Resilience*. In Cameron, K., Dutton, J. E., & Quinn, R. E. (Eds), *Positive Organizational Scholarship*. San Francisco: Berrett-Koehler (pp. 94–110).

Tenório Junior, N. N., & Bjorn, P. (2019). Online Harassment in the Workplace: the Role of Technology in Labour Law Disputes. *Computer Supported Cooperative Work (CSCW), 28.* doi:10.1007/s10606-019-09351-2

Tessian. (2020). *Securing the future of hybrid working*. Retrieved from https://www.tessian.com/research/the-future-of-hybrid-working/

Todt, G., Weiss, M., & Hoegl, M. (2018). Mitigating negative side effects of innovation project terminations: The role of resilience and social support. *Journal of Product Innovation Management, 35*, 518–542.

Trump, B. D., Hossain, K., & Linkov, I. (2020). *Cybersecurity and Resilience in the Arctic*. Amsterdam: IOS Press.

Utz, S., & Kramer, N. (2009). The privacy paradox on social network sites revisited: The role of individual characteristics and group norms. *Cyberpsychology: Journal of Psychosocial Research on Cyberspace, 3*(2).

Vanhove, A. J., Herian, M. N., Perez, A. L. U., Harms, P. D., & Lester, P. B. (2016). Can resilience be developed at work? A meta-analytic review of resilience-building programme effectiveness. *Journal of Occupational and Organizational Psychology, 89*(2), 278–307. doi:https://doi.org/10.1111/joop.12123

Villiers, P. (2009). *Police and Policing: An Introduction*. Hook: Waterside Press.

Whitty, M. (2018). Do You Love Me? Psychological Characteristics of Romance Scam Victims. *Cyberpsychology, Behavior, and Social Networking, 21*(2), 105–109. doi:10.1089/cyber.2016.0729

Williams, T. A., Gruber, D. A., Sutcliffe, K. M., Shepherd, D. A., & Zhao, E. Y. (2017). Organizational response to adversity: Fusing crisis management and resilience research streams. *The Academy of Management Annals, 11*(2), 733–769. doi:10.5465/annals.2015.0134

Wood, D. D., & Hollnagel, E. (2006). *Resilience Engineering: Concepts and Precepts*. Boca Raton, FL: CRC Press.

Yang, Y., & Danes, S. M. (2014). Resiliency and resilience process of entrepreneurs in new venture creation. *Entrepreneurship Research Journal, 5*, 1–30.

Zimmermann, V., & Renaud, K. (2019). Moving from a 'human-as-problem' to a 'human-as-solution' cybersecurity mindset. *International Journal of Human-Computer Studies, 131*, 169–187. doi:10.1016/j.ijhcs.2019.05.005

Culture $\quad$ 5

Context

Culture has been referred to as 'a slippery and ubiquitous concept' (Birukou, Blanzieri, Giorgini, & Giunchiglia, 2009). It is a concept that it could be argued people easily recognise but struggle to vocalise. This chapter discusses the cultures that exist in an organisation and the national culture(s) that the organisation exists within, along with sub-cultures that may influence how an individual behaves in relation to cybersecurity.

Organisational culture

As discussed throughout this text, humans are both the victims and instigators of cybercrime. This can create a multitude of challenges for organisations, in the form of both unintentional and intentional insider threats. For instance, AT&T employees took bribes to plant malware on the company's network, resulting in a data breach (Cimpanu, 2019). Part of the reason that organisations are at risk of cybercrime is that using internet technologies is a fundamental aspect of their business practice. Nine out of ten UK businesses and eight out of ten UK charities have some form of online presence, including bank accounts, customer data, or online payment processes (Department for Culture, Media and Sport, 2022). Even if an organisation protects itself from external online threats, it still likely employs individuals who themselves make use of the internet, and as such are a potential threat. An example of this would be the case of a member of the Air National Guard in the USA who was arrested in relation

DOI: 10.4324/9781003300359-5

to the leak of classified information from the US military (Matza, 2023). The information that was leaked included US assessments of the war between Russia and the Ukraine, and sensitive information about American allies including Egypt, South Korea, and the UAE. The information was shared on a Discord server used by people to discuss video games. It has been reported that the airman in question had been warned repeatedly about his handling of classified information, with prosecutors in his trial claiming that the airman 'simply did not care' about the instructions he received from his superiors (Halpert, 2023). It was also reported that the airmen would brag online about how he would violate rules on classified information. Following this incident, the Pentagon announced greater security controls to prevent similar incidents happening in future (Bowden, 2023). This example raises questions on how the culture of that organisation enabled this individual to become an insider threat, and why swifter action was not taken when he first breached security rules. It also demonstrates how challenging it can be to ensure that an organisation is secure – if a well-funded government agency with a high awareness of the importance of cybersecurity can experience such issues, then other organisations may face even greater struggles. Overall, the factors that contribute to the cybersecurity of an organisation have been termed information security culture (da Veiga, Astakhova, Botha, & Herselman, 2020).

The leadership of an organisation can have a strong influence on organisational culture (Carpenter & Roer, 2022). There is the stereotype of the CEO of large organisations as being confident to the point of arrogance and even to psychopathy (Babiak & Hare, 2006), something that social engineers have commented is a factor they exploit and use against such CEOs (Hadnagy, 2018; Radcliffe, 2023). It should be noted though that the relationship between leadership and personality is debated (Yukl, 2002). It can also be challenging to ascertain how much importance the leadership of an organisation place on cybersecurity. Given the frequent reports of cybersecurity breaches in the media it is hard to imagine that organisations are not aware of the potential damage caused by a cybersecurity breach. This damage is not limited to the financial, but can also include the reputation of the organisation. This can occur even if the actual data breach of the organisation is relatively harmless – for instance the knowledge that the IT system of a bank has been breached may cause concern amongst customers of that bank, even if customer data was not part of the breach. Indeed reputational damage is one of the top three cybersecurity concerns, along with data breaches and supply chain disruption (ISACA, 2022). Therefore, if questioned, the leadership of organisations may feel that they are expected to demonstrate that they recognise the importance of cybersecurity. In support of this, it has been stated that eight out of ten businesses report that cybersecurity is a high priority for their senior management. However, it was also noted there is a trend towards trusting and deferring details of cybersecurity approaches to IT staff and external providers, resulting in a lack of detailed understanding of cybersecurity within the leadership team. This type of attitude contributes to the perception of cybersecurity professionals that organisations often do not fully appreciate the threat posed by cybersecurity. Cybersecurity experts have noted that they often tell their organisational clients that hackers are already in their system (Frenkel, 2016), as this prompts the organisation to take cybersecurity measures in the system. This echoes the refrain mentioned in Chapter 1, namely that 'it is not if you get hacked, it is when you get hacked'.

A priority for many businesses is how they are perceived by their competitors, investors, customers, regulators, and their own employees. This is one reason why reputational damage from a cyber-attack is a major concern for many organisations. As with individuals, organisations engage in impression management, in which the organisation attempts to shape how it is seen both internally and externally. This is of course the basis of the public relations and marketing activities that organisations undertake, which includes how they aim to be seen by their own employees. Jones & Pittman (1982) identified five tactics of impression management – ingratiation (to be seen as likeable), self-promotion (to be seen as competent), exemplification (such as staying late at work, to be seen as dedicated), intimidation (to be seen as menacing), and supplication (to be seen as needy). The tactics used by an organisation will depend on the impression they want to project, which in turn is something that attackers may seek to exploit. For example, a charity is unlikely to want to use the impression management technique of intimidation but may use supplication, as part of their appeal for donations to help those in need. As such a social engineer may choose to frame their attack as a plea for help, as this would be consistent with the image the charity wishes to project. In their review of the research literature, Bolino, Long, and Turnley (2016) identify the impression management behaviours that are used by and within organisations, and assess the evidence base for them. They reported that ingratiation appeared to have mixed results, such as when an employee attempts to ingratiate themselves with a more senior member of the organisation. Whilst this may be initially successful, repeated use of ingratiation tactics can have a negative outcome. Similarly, the literature suggests self-promotion to appear competent may be an effective impression management tactic in some contexts but can come across as arrogance or bragging in other contexts. The authors give the example of the study by Cialdini (2001), who found that patients prefer it when doctors display their credentials and certificates on the wall of their waiting rooms. Again, such acts of impression management could be counterproductive – the information that individuals and organisations use to self-promote is the same information that attackers and social engineers will be able to exploit.

A challenge for organisations is the speed with which technology develops, and the complexity and fluidity of cyber-threats. This is something that smaller companies can find especially problematic, due to the lack of relevant resources and expertise (Fagbule, 2023). However, larger organisations are not immune to these struggles. Organisations have also reported receiving information and guidance about cybersecurity from a wide range of sources, with varying use of threat intelligence (Department for Culture, Media and Sport, 2022). These sources can include those provided by individuals in the cybersecurity community, such as Hackmageddon (https://www.hackmageddon.com), which records details of high profile cybersecurity breaches, and PhishTank (https://phishtank.org), which curates examples of phishing emails. The availability of this information is positive, although it should be considered how individuals and organisations navigate this information can help us understand what it is important to focus on. This can require a degree of expertise. However, as reported by ISACA, cybersecurity challenges are further compounded by the difficulties companies have experienced in retaining qualified cybersecurity staff, a situation that appears to have been exacerbated by the COVID-19 pandemic (ISACA, 2022). These staff losses are especially notable in midcareer employees aged 35 to 44, with burnout also being evident amongst cybersecurity staff. In addition, approximately two thirds of organisations reported that they have unfilled cybersecurity vacancies, with it often taking between three to six months to fill a post. The biggest skills gaps seen by employers, cited by 54% of them, are social skills around communication, flexibility, and leadership. In relation to the threat landscape, over half of organisations surveyed believed it to be likely or very likely that they would experience a cyber-attack in the coming year. However, it has also been noted that most organisations (82%) are confident in their ability to detect and respond to cyber-attacks, despite the gaps in recruitment. This once again highlights a disconnect between the reality of cybersecurity threats and what appears to be the overly optimistic view that organisations have about their ability to protect themselves. It was also found that 80% of organisations reported a positive impact from education and awareness programmes, although it could be queried how impact is measured and quantified in these cases. As will be discussed in Chapter 6, there can be a risk in assuming that an initial positive impact of cybersecurity training leads to meaningful, long-term change.

Further sub-types of insider threat have been proposed that go beyond the two broad categories of intentional and unintentional insider threat, such as the taxonomy proposed by the CERT National Insider Threat Center (Cappelli, Moore, & Trzeciak, 2012). The components of this taxonomy are as follows:

- Information Technology (IT) Sabotage: use of IT to direct specific harm toward an organization or an individual
- Intellectual Property (IP) Theft: purposely abusing one's credentials to steal confidential or proprietary information from the organization
- Entitled Independent: an insider acting primarily alone to steal information to take to a new job or to his/ her own side business
- Ambitious Leader: a leader of an insider crime who recruits insiders to steal information for some larger purpose
- Fraud: unauthorised modification, addition, or deletion of an organisation's data for personal gain, or theft of information that leads to an identity crime (e.g., identity theft, credit card fraud)

Following a review of the literature, Georgiadou, Mouzakitis, and Askounis (2021) proposed key indicators for different types of insider threats, as based on prior work by the CERT National Insider Threat Center (Cappelli et al., 2012). Dissatisfaction for example was identified in this model as being a possible motivating factor for becoming an insider threat. Both policy and roles awareness and situational awareness were found to be predictive of unintentional insider threat. This could suggest that a behaviour change campaign designed to address these points could reduce the risk of unintentional insider threat. However it has been reported that when surveyed most employees within an organisation will report that they understand cybersecurity policies and procedures, and yet will continue to make errors (Tessian, 2020). Indeed, it is interesting to note how few of the identified risk factors for insider threat are individual and malleable behaviours. For instance, if individual resilience is, as previous discussed, an innate personality trait, then it could be challenging to change this in individual employees. However, several of the identified insider threat indicators such as auditing, access control, and policy violations relate to both conceptualisations of resilience as a capability and a process, as well as organisational culture.

Implicit in many of the studies of organisation resilience of the type discussed in Chapter 4 – albeit often not directly stated – is the role of organisational culture. As with resilience, organisational culture is a complex construct that has been defined and conceptualised in a multitude of ways in the research literature, with a high number of diverse components identified that can influence the culture of an organisation. This broader organisational culture strongly influences the information security culture or the organisation, and in turn the cybersecurity behaviours and attitudes of members of that organisation (da Veiga, Astakhova, Botha, & Herselman, 2020; Hassan, Ismail, & Maarop, 2015; Mahfuth, Yussof, Abu Baker, & Ali, 2017). Aoyama, Naruoka, Koshijima, Machii, & Seki (2015) examined the role of leadership in resilience during a cyber incident handling task, in one of the limited examples of research that directly links a component of organisation culture to cyber resilience. Following observations taken during a cyber incident handling training event, the authors reported that:

A. Complete assigned tasks vs overtake new events: the execution of the original task is often interrupted by another event.
B. Miscommunication: communication between task groups and managers increases the frustration, and leads to misunderstandings. The communication path prepared for normal operations is not enough in a crisis. Being stuck in a communication path can affect critical decision making too. A predesigned protocol for communication is key to control the situation. Also, over-communication should be avoided.
C. Prevention vs detection vs response task priority: the resources of the team should be allocated to prevention, detection, and response tasks in a balanced way. It is notable that the allocation should not be static.
D. Fix big security hole vs protect the critical production path: defence teams have a tendency to focus on quick fixes of easily noticeable security holes. The management must conduct risk/ impact analysis to determine the significance to the production line. In addition, with limited resources in the team, sometimes there is not enough resources available to address two critical security breaches.
E. Ambiguous responsibility of role (assumption): this challenge is highly related to the game's nature. Even though the roles are given to each participant at the beginning of the exercise, the responsibility to complete the task is up to the team. Ambiguity of role definition leads to a gap or overlap between task groups. This challenge is linked to miscommunication.
F. Priority of entire game vs. priority of the moment: when the situation becomes intense, management often lose their ability to foresee the long-term goal.

The findings of Aoyama et al. (2015) are largely consistent with the conceptualisation of resilience discussed in the previous chapter, as in, they incorporate both short-term and long-term adversity, and highlight the importance of learning from past events and predicting future events. However, the findings also demonstrate the role of human factors in cyber resilience, and a system that is intended to be resilient can become derailed when human capacities and cognitions are not considered. The psychological factors that created issues in the training exercise observed by Aoyama et al. (2015) include attentional demands, cognitive overload, emotional arousal, role ambiguity, and decision making biases. Aoyama, Naruoka, Koshijima, and Watanabe (2015) discuss these findings in relation to the Context Control Model (COCOM), in which Hollnagel and Woods (2005) operationalised the concept of control. This model describes four control modes: strategic, tactical, opportunistic, and scrambled. Under the strategic control mode, several goals are tackled; there is abundant time available to meet these goals; there is the opportunity for an elaborate evaluation of the outcome; and actions are selected based on models and predictions. The tactical control mode has some similarities, but also greater constraints. The goals that the organisation is trying to achieve may be more limited; the time available may be adequate, but not abundant; there may be an opportunity for a detailed evaluation of the outcome; and actions are selected based on plans and previous experiences. Next, the opportunistic control mode can have one or two competing goals, with just adequate time to achieve these goals and the opportunity for a concrete evaluation of the outcome. In this control model, actions are selected based on habit and associations. Finally, in the scrambled control mode, the organisation is trying to achieve one goal, which might not be relevant to the required tasks. There is inadequate time to achieve this goal, the evaluation of the goal is rudimentary, and the selection of actions is random.

Aoyama, Naruoka, Koshijima, and Watanabe (2015) applied COCOM to the management of a defence team in a cyber handling incident, noting that the control style changes during an incident, often unintentionally, moving from strategic to scrambled. This occurs through several mechanisms. For example, in the strategic control mode there are fewer cases of role ambiguity, but as the control mode moves to opportunistic or scrambled there is greater role ambiguity, with individuals being unsure what their exact role should be in response to that incident. Similarly, miscommunication is rare in a strategic control mode, less rare in the tactical control mode, frequent in the opportunistic control mode, and confused in the scrambled control mode. This shift in behaviours and decision-making style under pressure is consistent with psychological research into cognition, specifically the use of heuristics and cognitive biases. As discussed in Chapter 2, this refers to when individuals make quick decisions based on limited information and prior assumptions. In doing so they are employing the cognitive miser approach, as opposed to the naïve scientist approach in which individuals make more comprehensive and rational decisions (Fiske & Taylor, 2008). The strategy that individuals use to determine which of these cognitive styles is most appropriate to the situation is referred to as being a motivated tactician (Kruglanski, 1996). It is interesting to note that cyber-attacks such as phishing emails and other social engineering attacks are designed to push the targets from a naïve scientist style of decision to a cognitive miser one (Montanez, Golob, & Xu, 2020), and in doing so increase the probability of human error occurring (Bullee, Montoya, Junger, & Hartel, 2017). As such it could be observed that there are parallels between the failure of cyber resilience at a micro, individual level, and the failure of cyber resilience at the macro, organisational level. It also suggests that behaviour change strategies that are designed to reduce susceptibility to social engineering attacks may be beneficial in promoting resilience in organisations, as there is a shared goal to encourage individuals to use the more comprehensive, naïve scientist approach towards decision making.

As commented, it is not only large companies who are the victims of cybercrime. It has been reported that start-up companies in the UK have been targeted by cyber-attacks, through the setting up of nearly identical websites and tricking employees with social engineering to make erroneous payments (Burgess, 2015). Whilst a small, start-up company may not have the same funds as a large company, the relative ease in which a social engineering attack can be conducted can mean that it is still a cost-effective strategy to target them. This is consistent with Routine Activities Theory (Cohen & Felson, 1979), in which an 'absence of capable guardianship' increases the likelihood of a victim being targeted by a criminal. This is because in the context of cybersecurity this concept of capable guardianship is often represented by information security specialists. A start-up company is less likely to have sufficiently qualified and experienced IT security staff who can protect against cyber-attack. This is also evident in small to medium sized enterprises (SMEs), where companies lack the time, money, and resources to invest in cybersecurity, despite fully understanding how important this is (Fagbule, 2023). In addition, it has been noted that there can be differences in approaches to cybersecurity in SMEs among different cultures. For instance, it has been noted that a barrier to cybersecurity in SMEs can include internal organisational cultural factors, budget, management support, and attitudes (Kabanda, Tanner, & Kent, 2018). Of course, as outlined in Chapter 1, very large and well-resourced companies are not immune to cyber-attacks, with many cases of high-profile technology companies falling victim.

It is interesting to note that some of the problems faced in organisations and businesses have parallels in cybercrime. One example of this is the malware known as ZeuS, amongst other names, which was created by a hacker who went by the name Slavik. ZeuS is one of the most widespread and damaging pieces of malware known to exist, and has been used to fraudulently gain access to bank accounts and to compromise companies including the Bank of America and NASA (Rhysider, 2022). Slavik took advantage of the growth of internet banking when it started to become mainstream in the late 2000s to introduce this malware into people's computers, where it would collect personal information, including bank account login details. However, the malware went further than that. It also turned any computer that it infected into being part of a botnet, meaning that computer would now be used to conduct further acts of cybercrime. It has been commented that Slavik chose the final name of ZeuS for the malware because he wanted it to be seen as the king of the bots, in the same way that Zeus is the king of the Greek gods in Greek mythology (Rhysider, 2022). Slavik approached his activities very much in the style of an entrepreneur setting up a business. He did not wish the ZeuS software to be something that people made use of once. Instead, he regularly updated it, adding in new features. He sold access to the malware online in underground forums, providing customer support for those users who wanted to use the botnet but lacked the skills to develop their own.

Slavik sought to diversify and maximise his income streams to ensure his cybercrime business would be robust, but he had a problem. Other hackers and cybercriminals were trying to resell their copies of ZeuS or were selling their own customised version but doing it under the ZeuS brand. As cybersecurity technology developed, Slavik found that he had to find new ways to handle the money that had been stolen from bank accounts. This involved the use of money mules – people to whom the stolen money could initially be transferred, who in turn would then pass it onto another account owned by the hackers, minus a small fee for the mule. This is of course money laundering, with mules being recruited through adverts placed online for working at home. Such adverts have been documented on social media platforms, such as Instagram (Bekkers, Moneva, & Leukfeldt, 2022). Hackers known as Gribodemon and Harderman then modified ZeuS into a new malware called SpyEye. The initial version of this was very poor compared to ZeuS, but was sold for only $400, as opposed to the over $8,000 that ZeuS was sold for. This created a power struggle, not dissimilar to that between two competing businesses. Then, unexpectedly, both Zeus and SpyEye announced that ZeuS was going to be merged with SpyEye. This led to speculation on what had happened, and whether for example Slavik had decided to retire (Rhysider, 2022). However, the merger never actually happened. Slavik then released ZeuS version 3, which came to be called Gameover ZeuS. This new version was Malware-as-a-Service (MaaS), delivered as a subscription-based service via the Cloud. Slavik was eventually identified as a Russian national, Evgeniy Mikhailovich Bogachev. At the time of writing, he remains at large, and is listed on the FBI's Cyber Most Wanted list (https://www.fbi.gov/wanted/cyber), with a $3 million reward for information leading to arrest and/or conviction. This case demonstrates one of the challenges identified in Chapter 1, which is that it is often difficult, or impossible, for individuals in some countries to be prosecuted by those from outside of that country. It would be intriguing to do research to better understand the organisational culture within the cybercrime ecosystem, although such work does of course present many challenges.

One way that organisations attempt to improve their organisational cybersecurity is by sending their own phishing emails internally, such as when the internet domain registry company GoDaddy employees were tested with a fake email about bonuses (Longhi, 2020). This does raise questions of how employees feel about being continually tested in this way, and the impact that this could have on organisational culture. Academic research has also been conducted on employee susceptibility to phishing emails (Kearney & Kruger, 2016), testing how effective the following phishing email would be when sent internally to members of a company, which included a deliberate misspelling in the company name in the link that the employees were asked to click on.

> *Due to unforeseen changes to our back-end security systems, we require you to validate your username and password today. Thank you to all of you who have already validated your details.*

It was found that 83% of respondents provided their username and password in response to this phishing email. The emotional and persuasive elements evident in the email include legitimacy (the source of the message is legitimate), authority (the message has been issued by someone with authority), scarcity (time to react is limited), and conformity (the belief that others have already completed the request). These are consistent with social psychological research and the types of exploits used by social engineers, as discussed in Chapter 2. Further discussion on behaviour change and prevention strategies will be provided in Chapter 6.

National culture

If trying to define the culture of an organisation is difficult, attempting to define culture on a national level is even more so. It is though necessary if the cybersecurity behaviours of both individuals and organisations are to be understood, as all these entities exist within a broader national culture. In some cases, they may be influenced by several cultures or, as in the case of multinational cooperations, must understand how to operate securely in multiple countries across the world. This is before even considering whether any single country has only a singular culture, or the role that online technologies may play in how people perceive themselves and interact with others. It has been noted that the internet can provide people with the opportunity to communicate and behave in ways that transcend that person's culture (Pflug, 2011). Cultural differences can be subtle and, to those outside of that culture, somewhat perplexing. For example, it was noted by Western media that China's President Xi had two cups of tea in front of him at the National People's Congress in China in 2023, something that was believed to be a deliberate act intended to convey power (Bubalo, 2023). These complexities and nuances of culture are something which need to be addressed when assessing cybersecurity threats and designing prevention and behaviour change strategies. It should also be noted how the increasing size of companies can begin to blur the lines between organisational and national culture – for instance in 2017 it was recorded that Walmart had a greater financial turnover than the country of Belgium (Belinchon & Moynihan, 2018).

Research highlights some of the ways that national culture can influence cybersecurity behaviours. For example, Selim (2019) observed that there is a relationship between culture and self-disclosure. That is, people in some cultures are more likely to share information about themselves to others than in other cultures. Many social engineering attacks contain an element of information gathering (open-source intelligence, or OSINT) about the targeted individual or organisation. As such individuals who more openly share information about themselves may be at greater risk of social engineering attacks. As was highlighted in Chapter 2, the information that is sought by social engineers is often that which, on the surface, can appear to be very trivial. However, as commented by Bragh, McKenna, and Fitzsimmons (2002) we should be cautious in making assumptions about the relationship between culture and self-disclosure on the internet, where anonymous communication is possible.

There have been several models proposed that have attempted to characterise the different components of culture. One of the first models of culture was that put forward by E. T. Hall (1976). This model describes culture in terms of high and low contexts, with context in this case referring to anything that shapes the communication within the culture, such as social norms, shared history, and the environment. A high culture context is one in which people tend to have close, long-standing relationships. Edward T. Hall and Mildred R. Hall (1990) identify Japan as being an example of one of the highest context cultures, commenting that people in that culture rarely say what they think and instead use 'a complex system of strategic politeness'. They also note that Germany is an example with a low context culture, where people are more direct in their communications. There is a lack of research on how (or if) social engineers and other cyber-adversaries tailor their attacks to the culture of the target, but it would seem likely that different strategies may be required for different context cultures. For instance, a more direct approach to information gathering (e.g., calling a company to query what PDF software they use, as per the example given in Chapter 2) may be more effective in Germany than Japan, as in the latter there could be more resistance to disclosing information to a stranger.

An alternative model is that put forward by Schwartz (2012), which proposes four cultural categories: openness to change, self-transcendence, self-enhancement, and conservation. Contained within these are 10 different dimensions, one of which is security. This refers more broadly to people's sense of security in terms of safety and well-being but does of course appear to be highly relevant to cybersecurity. Other dimensions in this model may also be relevant. For example, the dimension of power is something that could influence the success of phishing emails that are based on some expression of authority. This is typically done by framing the phishing email as being from some type of government organisation, such as the FBI or tax revenue, with a threat of legal action if the recipient does not click on a link or open an attached file. Similarly, the dimension of benevolence could influence how likely scams based on charity appear to be successful. It has been argued that the Schwartz model provides a fluid and detailed approach that recognises the overlap in cultural dimensions. Despite this, it does not appear to be a model that is widely used in the cybersecurity research literature.

Instead, the most popular cultural model that appears to be used in cybersecurity, and in business more broadly, is Hofstede's model (Hofstede, Hofstede, & Minkov, 2010). This model proposes six dimensions of culture, as follows:

- Power distance – how far the gap is between the people in power and the public.
- Individualism vs collectivism – whether people place emphasis on their individual well-being and success, or if they put more emphasis on the well-being and success of their friends, family, and wider community.
- Masculinity vs femininity – the extent to which traditional gender roles are present within the culture.
- Uncertainty avoidance – the degree of risk that a culture can tolerate, where a culture with high uncertainty avoidance will try to avoid doing anything that might have a risk.
- Long-term orientation – the extent to which a culture plans for the long-term future.
- Indulgence vs restraint – how much emphasis the culture places on having fun, which could also be considered in terms of how conservative a culture is.

As with the other cultural models, there is a lack of research into how the dimensions identified in Hofstede's model could be applied to cybersecurity beliefs and behaviours. Nevertheless, it is possible to speculate what some of the impacts might be. For instance, members of a culture that is high in uncertainty avoidance could be considered less likely to take risks in opening links in emails from unknown senders. Similarly, an organisation based in a culture with a high degree of long-term orientation could be expected to invest more time and resources into identifying future threats and ensuring that their cyber practices are safe and sustainable. However, there is a risk in making assumptions concerning the cause and effect of cultural dimensions on behaviour. As previously commented, cultural influences are complicated, and for many people are not limited to influence from a single culture. Indeed, the popularity of the Hofstede model may in part be due to its relative simplicity, along with the existence of online services that provide comparisons between countries and how they score on these dimensions (e.g. https://www.hofstede-insights.com/product/compare-countries/). The model has been criticised on several points, such as being based on samples within some countries (such as IBM employees) that are not representative of the general populations of those countries (Shaiq, Khalid, Akram, & Ali, 2011). Vignoles et al. (2016) also comment that the model does not capture the diversity within cultures, although this is a criticism that could be applied to other models of culture.

Overall, both organisational culture and national culture are important influences on behaviour in cybersecurity – not just the behaviour of the intended targets of cyber-attacks, but also those who are behind them. Organisational culture is something that organisations can, in theory, exert influence over to improve cybersecurity practices. Governments arguably have less direct influence over the national culture of a country, but there remains the potential for culture change to be introduced to reduce the harm caused by cyber-attacks. In the case of both organisational and national contexts however the challenge is the complexity of cultures, and the risk of unintended consequences from attempting to change these cultures. These issues of prevention and behaviour change are discussed in more depth in the next chapter.

References

Aoyama, T., Naruoka, H., Koshijima, I., Machii, W., & Seki, K. (2015). *Studying resilient cyber incident management from large-scale cyber security training.* Paper presented at the 10th Asian Control Conference (ASCC), Kota Kinabalu, Malaysia, May 31–Jun 03.

Aoyama, T., Naruoka, H., Koshijima, I., & Watanabe, K. (2015). *How management goes wrong? The human factor lessons learned from a cyber incident handling exercise.* Paper presented at the 6th International Conference on Applied Human Factors and Ergonomics (AHFE), Las Vegas, NV, July 26–30.

Babiak, P., & Hare, R. D. (2006). *Snakes in suits: When psychopaths go to work.* New York: Regan Books/Harper Collins Publishers.

Bekkers, L. M. J., Moneva, A., & Leukfeldt, E. R. (2022). Understanding cybercrime involvement: a quasi-experiment on engagement with money mule recruitment ads on Instagram. *Journal of Experimental Criminology.* doi:10.1007/s11292-022-09537-7

Belinchon, F., & Moynihan, Q. (2018). 25 giant companies that are bigger than entire countries. Retrieved from https://www.businessinsider.com/25-giant-companies-that-earn-more-than-entire-countries-2018-7?r=US&IR=T

Birukou, A., Blanzieri, E., Giorgini, P., & Giunchiglia, F. (2009). A Formal Definition of Culture. *Models for intercultural collaboration and negotiation.* doi:10.1007/978-94-007-5574-1_1

Bolino, M., Long, D., & Turnley, W. (2016). Impression Management in Organizations: Critical Questions, Answers, and Areas for Future Research. In Morgeson, F. P. (Ed.), *Annual Review of Organizational Psychology and Organizational Behavior, Vol. 3* (pp. 377–406).

Bowden, G. (2023). Pentagon to tighten controls after classified documents leak. Retrieved from https://www.bbc.co.uk/news/world-us-canada-66111469

Bragh, J. A., McKenna, K. Y. A., & Fitzsimmons, G. M. (2002). Can you see the real me? Activation and expression of the 'true self' on the Internet. *Journal of Social Issues, 58,* 33–48.

Bubalo, M. (2023). One man, two cups: Is President Xi's double tea a power move? Retrieved from https://www.bbc.co.uk/news/av/world-asia-china-64897273

Bullee, J.-W., Montoya, L., Junger, M., & Hartel, P. (2017). Spear phishing in organisations explained. *Information & Computer Security, 25*(5), 593–613. doi:10.1108/ICS-03–2017–0009

Burgess, M. (2015). UK tech start-ups hit by targeted 'insider' Phishing scam. *Wired.* Retrieved from https://www.wired.co.uk/article/hacking-start-up-email-london-phishing-attacks-money

Cappelli, D. M., Moore, A. P., & Trzeciak, R. F. (2012). *The CERT guide to insider threats: how to prevent, detect, and respond to information technology crimes (Theft, Sabotage, Fraud).* Boston, MA: Addison-Wesley.

Carpenter, P., & Roer, K. (2022). *The Security Culture Playbook: An Executive Guide To Reducing Risk and Developing Your Human Defense Layer.* Hoboken, N.J.: Wiley.

Cialdini, R. B. (2001). *Influence: Science and Practice.* Boston, MA: Pearson Education.

Cimpanu, C. (2019). AT&T employees took bribes to plant malware on the company's network. Retrieved from https://www.zdnet.com/article/at-t-employees-took-bribes-to-plant-malware-on-the-companys-network/

Cohen, L. E., & Felson, M. (1979). Social Change and Crime Rate Trends: A Routine Activity Approach. *American Sociological Review, 44*(4), 588–608. doi:10.2307/2094589

da Veiga, A., Astakhova, L. V., Botha, A., & Herselman, M. (2020). Defining organisational information security culture—Perspectives from academia and industry. *Computers & Security, 92.* doi:10.1016/j.cose.2020.101713

Department for Culture, Media and Sport. (2022). *Cyber Security Breaches Survey 2022.* Retrieved from https://www.gov.uk/government/statistics/cyber-security-breaches-survey-2022/cyber-security-breaches-survey-2022

Fagbule, O. (2023). *Cyber Security Training in Small to Medium-sized Enterprises (SMEs): Exploring Organisation Culture and Employee Training Needs.* PhD, Bournemouth University.

Fiske, S. T., & Taylor, S. E. (2008). *Social cognition: from brains to culture* (1st edn). Boston, MA: McGraw-Hill Higher Education.

Frenkel, S. (2016). Cybersecurity is broken and the hacks are going to just keep coming. Retrieved from https://www.buzzfeednews.com/article/sheerafrenkel/cybersecurity-is-broken-and-the-hacks-are-going-to-just-keep#.uyXvzzB81

Georgiadou, A., Mouzakitis, S., & Askounis, D. (2021). Detecting insider threat via a cyber-security culture framework. *Journal of Computer Information Systems,* 1–11. doi:10.1080/08874417.2021.1903367

Hadnagy, C. (2018). *Social Engineering: The Science of Human Hacking.* Indianapolis, IN: Wiley.

Hall, E. T. (1976). *Beyond Culture.* New York: Anchor Books.

Hall, E. T., & Hall, M. R. (1990). *Understanding cultural differences.* Yarmouth, ME: Intercultural Press.

Halpert, M. (2023). Suspected Pentagon leaker was warned multiple times, prosecutors say. Retrieved from https://www.bbc.co.uk/news/world-us-canada-65625524

Hassan, N. H., Ismail, Z., & Maarop, N. (2015). Information security culture: A systematic literature review. In Jamaludin, Z. ChePa, N., Ishak, W. H. W., & Zaibon S. B. (Eds), *Proceedings of the 5th International Conference on Computing & Informatics* (pp. 456–463).

Hofstede, G. H., Hofstede, G. J., & Minkov, M. (2010). *Cultures and organizations: Software of the mind* (3rd edn). New York: McGraw-Hill.

Hollnagel, E., & Woods, D. D. (2005). *Joint cognitive systems: foundations of cognitive systems engineering.* Boca Raton, FL: Taylor & Francis.

ISACA. (2022). *State of Cybersecurity 2022: Global Update on Workforce Efforts, Resources and Cyberoperations.* Retrieved from https://www.isaca.org/go/state-of-cybersecurity-2022

Jones, E. E., & Pittman, T. (1982). Toward a general theory of strategic self-presentation. In Suls, J. (Ed.), *Psychological Perspectives on the Self.* Hillsdale, N.J.: Lawrence Erlbaum Associates.

Kabanda, S., Tanner, M., & Kent, C. (2018). Exploring SME cybersecurity practices in developing countries. *Journal of Organizational Computing and Electronic Commerce, 28,* 269–282. doi:10.1080/10919392.2018.1484598

Kearney, W. D., & Kruger, H. A. (2016). Can perceptual differences account for enigmatic information security behaviour in an organisation? *Computers & Security, 61,* 46–58. doi:http://dx.doi.org/10.1016/j.cose.2016.05.006

Kruglanski, A. W. (1996). Motivated social cognition: principles of the interface. In Higgins, E. T., & Kruglanski, A. W. (Eds), *Social Psychology: Handbook of Basic Principles.* New York: Guilford Press.

Longhi, L. (2020). GoDaddy Employees Were Told They Were Getting a Holiday Bonus. It Was Actually a Phishing Test. Retrieved from https://coppercourier.com/story/godaddy-employees-holiday-bonus-secruity-test/

Mahfuth, A., Yussof, S., Abu Baker, A., & Ali, N. (2017). A systematic literature review: Information security culture. In *2017 5th International Conference on Research and Innovation in Information Systems.*

Matza, M. (2023). Jack Teixeira: New charges for airman over leaked documents. Retrieved from https://www.bbc.co.uk/news/world-us-canada-65923978

Montanez, R., Golob, E., & Xu, S. H. (2020). Human cognition through the lens of social engineering cyberattacks. *Frontiers in Psychology, 11.* doi:10.3389/fpsyg.2020.01755

Pflug, J. (2011). Contextuality and computer-mediated communication: a cross cultural comparison. *Computers in Human Behavior, 27*(1), 131–137. doi:https://doi.org/10.1016/j.chb.2009.10.008

Radcliffe, J. (2023). *People Hacker: Confessions of a Burglar for Hire.* London: Simon & Schuster.

Rhysider, J. (2022). ZeuS. *Darknet Diaries.* Retrieved from https://darknetdiaries.com/episode/111/

Schwartz, S. H. (2012). An overview of the Schwartz theory of basic values. *Online Readings in Psychology and Culture, 2*(1). Retrieved from http://dx.doi.org/10.9707/2307-0919.1116

Selim, H. (2019). Cultural Considerations on Online Interactions. In Attrill-Smith, A., Fullwood, C., Keep, M., & Kuss, D. J. (Eds), *Oxford Handbook of Cyberpsychology.* Oxford: Oxford University Press.

Shaiq, H. M. A., Khalid, H. M. S., Akram, A., & Ali, B. N. H. (2011). Why not everybody loves Hofstede? What are the alternative approaches to study of culture? *European Journal of Business and Management, 3,* 101–111.

Tessian. (2020). *Securing the future of hybrid working.* Retrieved from https://www.tessian.com/research/the-future-of-hybrid-working/

Vignoles, V. L., Owe, E., Becker, M., Smith, P. B., Easterbrook, M. J., Brown, R., . . . Bond, M. H. (2016). Beyond the 'east-west' dichotomy: Global variation in cultural models of selfhood. *Journal of Experimental Psychology: General, 145*(8), 966–1000. doi:10.1037/xge0000175

Yukl, G. (2002). *Leadership in organisations.* Upper Saddle River, N.J.: Prentice Hall.

Behaviour change and prevention

6

Context

Having established the range of factors that may cause and influence cybercrime, the next step is to consider how to address these challenges. Whilst there are technological approaches that can improve cybersecurity, it is ultimately human behaviour that determines the safety of socio-technical systems. Excluding the debateable case of artificial intelligence, which will be discussed in Chapter 7, all cases of cyber-attack require some element of action and decision-making by the attacker. Most cyber-attacks also require the victim to do something, such as clicking on a link in a phishing email or divulging sensitive information in some way. As such, robust cybersecurity requires an understanding of behaviour. This is where psychology research can make a significant contribution. There are decades of research from psychology and other social science areas that can be used to not only understand how and why people act and interact in different ways and make different decisions, but can inform us how to change human behaviour. Social psychologists consider the nature of interactions between individuals and groups; investigative psychologists consider choice of victim and different types of offending; cognitive psychologists study decision making, heuristics and biases; and forensic psychologists may attempt to reduce future offending, for example. This encompasses other concepts used in psychology such as prevention and harm reduction. These concepts can overlap, and in real-world practice may not have a clear distinction. Prevention refers to the strategy of preventing harm from occurring in the first place. An example of this would be how governments encouraged and/ or mandated citizens to wear face masks during the COVID-19 pandemic, to prevent those individuals

DOI: 10.4324/9781003300359-6

from becoming infected. However, wearing masks and other preventative measures such as hand washing only reduced the spread of the virus, they did not eliminate the risk. As such these measures could also be thought of as harm reduction. Other examples of harm reduction would include strategies such as ensuring that there are licensed taxis available at a taxi rank on weekend nights in city centres, on the basis that this will reduce the risk of individuals who have been drinking alcohol from driving home. There is an underlying acceptance in this approach that it is unrealistic to expect complete behaviour to occur, i.e., for people to not drink alcohol in pubs and clubs at weekends. As such, the focus becomes what can be done to lessen some of the risks. Finally, behaviour change involves techniques that are designed to change the behaviours of the target population. An example of this would be public health campaigns that seek to prompt people to give up smoking. In this case the goal is complete behaviour change, and not harm reduction – it would be very unusual for a health authority to promote the message that some smoking is ok. Nevertheless, there are often elements of prevention, harm reduction, and behaviour change in any campaign that seeks to address some type of problem that is at least partly caused by human behaviour. For instance, the wearing of masks during COVID-19 may be seen as primarily a preventative and harm reduction measure, but to occur it needed the target to also change their behaviour.

These concepts of behaviour change, harm reduction, and prevention can also be blurred within cybersecurity. If, as discussed in previous chapters, it is a case of 'when you get hacked, not if you get hacked' then the concept of prevention is not applicable. After all, if being victimised is inevitable then there is no point in devoting time and resources into preventing this from happening. Instead, the only option would appear to be harm reduction, where attempts are made to lessen the risk and the subsequent harm it may cause. This reflects the concept of target hardening in security, which refers to the idea of making a potential target less desirable to an attacker by making it harder to conduct an attack, such in the case of how residential properties can be made to be less appealing to burglars (Montoya, Junger, & Ongena, 2016). Drew (2020) further notes that target hardening in cybersecurity can take the form of self-protective behaviours, such as learning not to disclose sensitive information to seemingly appropriate external parties (a common technique used by social engineers) unless their identity has been clearly established. It is also supported by Routine Activities Theory (Cohen & Felson, 1979), which states that a target is at greater risk when it is attractive to the attacker. In other words, the attacker may be encouraged to attack someone else instead of you if they perceive that other target to be weaker. This does not of course stop the problem, but rather just moves the problem to someone else. In criminological terms this is a form of crime displacement (Hesseling, 2006). This argument suggests that if an area is flooded with police officers or CCTV, offenders may displace their criminal activity and move it elsewhere. Similarly, if a company has secure systems, or an individual does not easily disclose information, the attacker may simply move somewhere else. However as discussed in Chapter 3 there is often frustration amongst hackers and cybersecurity practitioners that large and well-resourced companies have very basic flaws in their cybersecurity. As such this concept of target hardening is a useful one. Nevertheless, prevention remains something that organisations are invested in. There may be a public relationship element to this – after all, organisations may not want to admit to their customers or members that they have accepted that it is inevitable they will experience cyber-breaches. In this book we broadly separate our discussion of the research literature into that relating to behaviour change (i.e., addressing problematic cyber behaviours which are already occurring) and that relating to prevention (i.e., efforts to prevent problematic cyber behaviours from developing in the first place).

Behaviour change

A key finding from the research literature on cybersecurity behaviour change is that providing security alone is insufficient to increase awareness or change behaviour (Bada, Sasse, & Nurse, 2015). This highlights the point that threat messages alone are not an adequate technique for encouraging individuals and organisations to protect themselves, as would appear to be the assumption of various official bodies (Williams, 2012). Instead, as Bada and Nurse (2019) argue from their review of the literature, there is a need to provide organisations with simple and practical advice that is relevant to the organisation's mission and resources. It has also been noted that it is important to have measurement tools that record both behaviour change and compliance (Bada et al., 2015). This reflects a behaviour change challenge that exists across all domains – simply asking the target population if they have changed their behaviour is unlikely to be a robust measure of whether behaviour change has actually occurred. In the case of an organisation for example, employees may not wish to admit their behaviour has not changed following cybersecurity training because they do not wish to be penalised.

If cyber resilience of the type discussed in Chapter 4 is lacking in an organisation, or if resilient behaviours and attitudes are not evident when the organisation is under attack, then change must occur. Such attempts to bring about change are often referred to in the literature as behaviour change as an umbrella term, but this is done with the knowledge that attitudes, cognitions, and emotions are components of behaviour and behaviour change strategies.

The concept of behaviour change to improve cybersecurity is of course a broad topic and a recognised challenge in the field. It is also an issue that, from a computing and IT perspective, often takes the aforementioned position of viewing humans as being the problem rather than part of the solution (Zimmermann & Renaud, 2019). However, much of the behaviour change literature that has been applied to cybersecurity is based upon studies from social and health psychology, which typically take a more holistic approach in which the idiosyncrasies of human behaviour are acknowledged and understood (Adams, Costa, Jung, & Choudhury, 2015). Adams et al. (2015) also observe that most behaviour change approaches in human computer interactions rely on what he terms the 'reflective mind', where the person is assumed to think carefully and deeply about cyber behaviours. This relates to the previously discussed concept of heuristics and cognitive biases and raises an important point when considering research into cyber behaviour change. It may be that the behaviour change strategies typically used within cybersecurity assume individuals are using a naïve scientist cognitive style (i.e., rational and contemplative) when the cyber-attack itself is pushing the targets to the cognitive miser style of decision-making (i.e., quick and superficial).

Despite the extensive evidence base for behaviour change in health and social psychology there are methodological and theoretical issues to consider when applying this knowledge to cybersecurity. Davis, Campbell, Hildon, Hobbs, and Michie (2015) argue that many behaviour change interventions reported in the literature may claim to be based on a theory, but that in many studies the application of the theory is poorly done. This is similar to the comment of Michie, van Stralen, and West (2011), who observe that behaviour change interventions often appear to be based on what the creators of the intervention believe to be a common-sense approach, rather than being based heavily on psychological theory. Davis et al. (2015) found that 82 different theories have been found in the behaviour change research literature, across a range of behavioural domains. Of these theories four were found to be the most widely used: the Transtheoretical Model of Change (Prochaska, Johnson, & Lee, 2009); the Theory of Planned Behaviour (Ajzen, 1991); Social Cognitive Theory (Bandura, 2003); and the Information-Motivation-Behavioural-Skills Model (Fisher & Fisher, 1996).

There is overlap between these theories, and elements in each that would appear to be relevant to cyber resilience. The Transtheoretical Model of Change (Prochaska et al., 2009) states that behaviour change occurs through a series of steps, including pre-contemplation, contemplation, preparation, action, and maintenance. This linear and sequential approach may be desirable to organisations who wish to bring about behaviour change in an ordered manner. However, the model does assume that no further action is required once the desired change is achieved. This may not be advisable in the case of cyber threats, where the nature of the attacks and the attackers are continually evolving. The Theory of Planned Behaviour states that behaviour is a result of attitudes, subjective norms, perceived behavioural control, and intention. This concept of perceived behavioural control fits with the aforementioned research that has linked locus of control (the degree to which individuals perceive they have control over their own actions) to cyber resilience. It also relates to the COM-B model of behaviour change (Michie et al., 2011) which, as shall be discussed, argues that behaviour is influenced by the capability and opportunity that the individual perceives themselves to have. Finally, the Theory of Planned Behaviour differentiates between the intention an individual has to conduct a behaviour and the actual execution of the behaviour. As shall be discussed further, this could be an important distinction, given the research evidence that suggests that cyber behaviour change campaigns that are successful in raising awareness and knowledge do not subsequently produce behaviour change. Social Cognitive Theory (Bandura, 2003) also includes capability as a component, although it differentiates this from perceived self-efficacy, which relates to how much an individual perceives themselves to be able to change their behaviour. It is important to highlight that the individual's perception may not match their actual ability, and indeed many behaviour change campaigns that are based upon Social Cognitive Theory aim to persuade the target audience that they have more control over their own actions than they may perceive. Finally, the Information-Motivation-Behavioural-Skills Model states that behaviour is a result of the skills, knowledge, and motivation of the individual. Whilst this model was developed to understand health behaviours it may be applicable to cybersecurity behaviours, particularly given the move towards describing protective cybersecurity behaviours in terms of cyber hygiene (Ncubukezi, Mwansa, & Rocaries, 2020). Cyber hygiene refers to the practices and steps that individuals can take to ensure that a computer system remains healthy and safe (Kioskli, Fotis, Nifakos, & Mouratidis, 2023). This rephrasing of cybersecurity could be considered an attempt to encourage individuals to see cybersecurity as a more personal issue that they have an investment in, as opposed to something that it is solely the responsibility of the IT department to deal with. It may also help encourage the application of the extensive evidence base from health psychology research to behaviour change challenges within cybersecurity, although this remains to be seen. As an observation, it does seem that the cybersecurity profession – or at least those people whose background is primarily in computing – do not fully appreciate the knowledge and expertise that can be provided by psychology. This is in part due to the misconceptions that those from computing backgrounds have about psychology, as has been noted in relation to the education of students who are completing computing degrees (Taylor-Jackson et al., 2020).

Bada et al. (2015) identified the psychological theories that have been used to inform cybersecurity behaviour change. Both the Theory of Planned Behaviour and Social Cognitive Theory were found to be used within this literature. In addition, the Theory of Reasoned Action (Ajzen & Fishbein, 1980) was identified as having been used as the theoretical basis for cyber behaviour change. The Theory of Reasoned Action is closely linked to the Theory of Planned Behaviour and argues that individuals have an internal decision mechanism in which the formation of intention of behaviour immediately precedes the same behaviour and mediates between that and the impact of other variables. According to this theory, the psychological requirements of intended behaviour are attitudes and perceived social norms. This inclusion of perceived social norms is relevant to organisational culture, as it suggests that individual behaviour is strongly influenced by what those individuals perceive to be the norm amongst their peers. Bada et al. (2015) also noted that Protection Motivation Theory (Rogers, 1975) was cited as the basis for some cyber behaviour change strategies. This theory states that whether an individual takes action to protect themselves is determined by i) how severe they perceive a threat to be and ii) how capable they perceive themselves to be in coping with that threat. As such the theory has overlap with the concepts of capability and self-efficacy contained within other psychological theories that have been used as the basis for cyber behaviour change strategies. Johnston, Warkentin, and Siponen (2015) note that when applying Protection Motivation Theory to cybersecurity behaviours that it is important to educate individuals on how to take the steps needed to protect themselves. In other words, if you present the target population with information about a threat you must also provide a clear explanation of the steps that can be taken to avoid that threat. This is consistent with the discussions on victimology and resilience in Chapter 4.

The Nudge Theory approach has also become a popular behaviour change strategy in recent years. It aims to change behaviour by steering people towards a desired choice, without actually removing the choice (Thaler & Sunstein, 2009). In doing so it may potentially increase an individual's sense of the control they have over their actions, which is pertinent to the concept of locus of control included within several other behaviour change theories. An advantage of the nudge literature is that it often includes practical examples of how the theory can be applied, and indeed could be argued to be more practitioner focussed than other theories of behaviour change. Caraban, Karapanos, Gonçalves, and Campos (2019) observes that the nudge approach has become popular in human-computer interaction (HCI) but is sometimes applied inappropriately. In their review of the application of nudge theory in HCI, Caraban et al. found 23 mechanisms for nudging grouped across six overall categories:

- Facilitate – default options, opt-out policies, positioning, hiding, suggesting alternatives

- Confront – throttling mindless activity, reminding of the consequences, creating friction, providing multiple viewpoints
- Deceive – adding inferior alternatives, biasing the memory of past experiences, placebos, deceptive visualisations
- Social influence – invoking feelings of reciprocity, leveraging public commitment, raising the visibility users' actions, enabling social comparison
- Fear – making resources scarce, reducing the distance
- Reinforce – just in time prompts, ambient feedback, instigating empathy, subliminal priming

These categories provide multiple ways in which cybersecurity may be improved. For instance, suggesting alternative versions of a password chosen by a user could help address the issue of users choosing a password that is memorable but not complicated enough for the system requirements (e.g., suggesting to a user that their password be 'Gr33nfly!' rather than 'Greenfly'). Despite sounding rather menacing, the mechanism of throttling mindless activity can be effective through prompting individuals to stop and think about an action before proceeding, especially when they may be acting without much conscious thought. An example given by Konstantinou, Caraban, and Karapanos (2019) is a system that curbs the unintentional spread of fake news by presenting social media users with a notification of the type 'We estimate a 90% chance of the article containing false information. Are you sure you want to publish this tweet?'. In doing so the individual is encouraged to act more as a naïve scientist (e.g., rational, in-depth thinking) rather than a cognitive miser (i.e., coming to quick conclusions). Similarly, the use of friction in a socio-technical system could be something simple such as a prompt for confirmation that appears onscreen when a user attempts to click on a link in an email that has originated from outside that organisation. There are examples in the research literature of the nudge approach in cybersecurity contexts. Harbach, Hettig, Weber, and Smith (2014) for example applied Nudge Theory to the downloading of smartphone apps, to help users understand why giving permissions to apps could be dangerous.

There are other mechanisms used in the nudge approach that have the potential to be applicable to cybersecurity, although as with any behaviour change strategy, consideration should be given to potential unintended consequences. As previously discussed, fear can be used as a nudge by increasing the perception that people have of cyber-attacks being a real and genuine threat, but only providing a sense of fear with no information about how to avoid a threat can be counterproductive. Gutek and Winter (1990) also argue that fear appeals which create too much emotional arousal impact negatively on user performance. Social influence can be a powerful factor in shaping behaviour, as discussed in relation to organisational culture in Chapter 5. However, there can be risks in the inappropriate application of nudge mechanisms based on social influence. For instance, enabling social comparisons may be beneficial when encouraging the employees of an organisation to compete on tasks that every employee has an equal and fair chance to achieve. However publicly sharing comparisons of which employees have been the victim of a phishing email may not engender positive staff morale and conflicts with the idea that it is impossible for any organisation to completely avoid cyber-attacks. Similarly, nudge mechanisms based on deception may be effective but may not be welcomed by the employees of that company. In general people do not respond well to what they perceive to be attempts to manipulate their behaviour (Steindl, Jonas, Sittenthaler, Traut-Mattausch, & Greenberg, 2015).

Finally, the COM-B model (Michie et al., 2011) provides an approach for understanding what needs to be in place for behaviour change to be effective. It argues that three components must be present: capability, opportunity, and motivation. In this model capability and opportunity influence the relationship between motivation and behaviour, rather than the behaviour itself. This model also states that capability and opportunity influence motivation, in that if individuals believe that they can perform an action then they will be motivated to do so. Conversely, if a behaviour is perceived to be difficult to achieve then the individual will feel less motivated to try to do so. In addition, both positive and negative feedback cycles can develop, in which for example experience may develop an individual's skill level (capability), and in doing so increase their motivation for a task. Similarly, if an individual does not have any ability to change capability or opportunity, such as in a homeostatic system, then their motivation to engage in a behaviour may decrease. Finally, the model states that individuals may have the capability and opportunity to execute a high number of behaviours in any given situation but will tend to only consider a small number of these. This choice may be made consciously or unconsciously. A consequence of this is that an individual may feel more motivated to make an incorrect choice, simply because it is more familiar or habitual. As such, compared to all the other behaviour change theories discussed, the COM-B model is the one that most closely includes the concept of the cognitive miser and naïve scientist forms of decision making, which respectively refer to quick, largely instinctive decision making opposed to more reasoned and comprehensive decision making.

COM-B differentiates between interventions (activities aimed at changing behaviour) and policies (actions on the part of responsible authorities that enable or support interventions). This has been incorporated into the Behaviour Change Wheel (Michie, van Stralen, & West, 2011). By including policies as part of the Behaviour Change Wheel, COM-B could be argued to be the most closely aligned behaviour model to organisational culture. For example, by including policies such as fiscal measures the model acknowledges one of the constraints that small to medium businesses often experience when making decisions on cybersecurity practices, namely money and resources (Fagbule, 2023). Similarly, the Behaviour Change Wheel includes legislation as a policy category. Culture and behaviour are in part shaped by legislation. Whilst there are some international legal conventions, such as the General Data Protection Regulations in the European Union, there are no universal laws that relate to the rights of internet users. Halder (2022) suggests that rights in cyberspace can be classed into two categories – the rights of users in cyberspace, and the rights of the victims of cybercrime. These can be considered in terms of freedom of speech, the right to privacy, the right to be protected against crimes, and the right to justice. Freedom of speech is a topic that is particularly subject to debate on the internet. This right may be evoked by those who want to be free to engage in hate speech or cyberbullying. As Halder (2022) comments, the legalities around these issues can be complex.

In a review of cyber behaviour change campaigns Bada et al. (2015) identified several reasons why cybersecurity behaviour change campaigns fail:

- Solutions are not aligned to business risks.
- Neither progress nor value are measured.
- Incorrect assumptions are made about people and their motivations.
- Unrealistic expectations are set.
- The correct skills are not deployed.
- Awareness is just background noise.

These factors are consistent with theories of behaviour change, in particular concepts of capability, self-efficacy, opportunity and motivation, as described in the Theory of Planned Behaviour (Ajzen, 1991) and COM-B (Michie et al., 2011). Issues such as unrealistic expectations and correct skills not being deployed are linked to the types of organisational culture factors discussed in Chapter 5. The findings by Bada et al. (2015) highlight the conflict that can occur between how behaviour change campaigns should be implemented – as based on the research evidence – and how they are actually implemented within the constraints of a busy organisation.

Overall, theories of behaviour and behaviour change are diverse and multi-faceted. There is no single theory that could be identified as being dominant; nor is there sufficient evidence within the cyber behaviour change literature to be able to say that any one theory is superior to the others for being used as the basis for intervention strategies. However, it is evident that there are some shared elements between the theories that may be relevant to cyber behaviour change strategies. This includes the psychological constructs of control, capability (self-efficacy), and motivation. In addition, the opportunities available to individuals to implement changes appear to be an important factor and relate to organisational culture factors around autonomy in the systems in which the individual operates. There would also appear to be links between behaviour change theories and resilience. As discussed, the key concept in cyber resilience of discouraging individuals from making hasty or unconscious decisions in the face of a cyber threat is consistent with behaviour change theories that promote a more conscious and reflective decision style. It could also be argued that the concepts of capability and self-efficacy are highly relevant to resilience – if a resilient individual is one who positively adapts in response to adversity, then the individual needs to believe in the first place that adaptation is possible. However, it must be acknowledged that these potential linkages between resilience and behaviour change are largely speculative. There appears to have been little discussion in the literature about the connection between resilience and behaviour change, despite their overlap in relation to being concerned with real world challenges.

The style in which the training is delivered may also be a factor in behaviour change, especially if this is not suitable for the target audience. For example, Taylor et al. (2017) reported that teaching psychology to computing students can be quite different from teaching psychology students, in that computing students:

- Place more emphasis on problem solving, logical thinking and future earning;
- Are less likely to consider the role of people in problem solving; and
- Expect there to be single, universally agreed explanations of psychological phenomena.

It is feasible to assume that similar barriers may exist in introducing cybersecurity training in a workplace. That is, individuals who work in the more technology focussed areas of the business may struggle to engage with training that takes a more person-centred approach, even if greater knowledge of human factors is an important part of that training. This is consistent with the position of Lee, Kiesler, and Forlizzi (2011), who argue that many behaviour change interventions used in cybersecurity are information-centric. As such, they assume that people fail to change their cyber behaviour because they do not have the knowledge of how to do so. This is consistent with some elements of behaviour change theories, such as the capability component of the COM-B. However, it does not account for other common elements of behaviour change theories, such as the need for the individual to be motivated. This view is echoed by Drew (2020) who observes, in relation to cybercrime victimisation prevention, that giving individuals more knowledge about cyber threats does not necessarily lead to a change in behaviour.

Discussing social engineering attacks, Hadnagy (2018) recommends four steps to creating a mitigation and prevention plan:

- Learn to identify social engineering attacks.
- Develop actionable and realistic policies.
- Perform regular real-world check-ups.
- Implement appliable security-awareness programmes.

These steps could be viewed as practical examples of how to develop resilience at an organisational level, or at least resilience to social engineering attacks. The steps refer to identifying adversity and taking positive steps to prevent and mitigate this adversity, which is consistent with the conceptualisation of resilience. As with behaviour change campaigns based on academic research however there may be challenges in implementing these approaches in real-world settings. Nevertheless, we would argue that the recommendations put forward by experts with lived experience such as Hadnagy (2018) and Radcliffe (2023) are highly valuable, and provide insights that cannot necessarily be gained from the academic research literature.

As discussed in Chapter 5 in relation to organisational culture, organisations vary in terms of the resources and skills they have in relation to cybersecurity. It could be argued that much of the research literature has focussed on cybersecurity behaviour change in large organisations. In response to this, Bada and Nurse (2019) identify five key points from the literature on cybersecurity in small and medium-sized enterprises (SMEs). Firstly, they note that it is vital that there is a good security culture in the SME. This is of course a point that applies to all organisations, as discussed in Chapter 5. Secondly, the cybersecurity education programme needs to align with the SME's resources. In other words, a cybersecurity programme that is comprehensive and effective in large organisations may be of little use if the resources it requires for successful implementation are beyond that of an SME. Thirdly, it is important to identify the important assets within the SME and understanding the harms that could be caused by a breach of those assets. This demonstrates a key aspect of cybersecurity risk – SMEs can hold data (such as customer bank details) that are as sensitive as that which a much larger organisation can hold. Fourthly, there is a need for governments to be involved in assisting SMEs in cybersecurity. Governments can provide resources and information, as well as setting basic security goals, such as the Cyber Essential scheme that is operated in the UK. Finally, there is a need for better communication and engagement with SMEs.

Prevention

As discussed, it can be difficult to truly discuss prevention in the context of cybersecurity, as this term presumes that the problem is not already occurring. However, there can be opportunities in socio-technical systems to bring about changes that may prevent cyber-risks from becoming more severe. A range of technological approaches have been developed for this, which incorporate machine learning, the use of personalised and user-specific sign in processes, two-factor authentication, and the creation of lists of known phishing sites (Iuga, Nurse, & Erola, 2016). Organisations can also make use of various systems to monitor employee and customer behaviour online and will note any unusual behaviour which may be indicative of a cybersecurity breach. This is likely an important factor in preventing some instances of cybercrime, although cybercriminals are aware of this and attempt to find alternative ways to achieve their goals (Rhysider, 2022). Nevertheless, monitoring of this type contributes to the target hardening of the organisation, meaning that the attackers may decide to focus on a different target who are not as efficient in their monitoring. It may be expected that being a victim of cybercrime in the past would be a preventative factor in becoming a victim of crime in future, as the individual should be better equipped to identify risks and take preventative actions. Drew (2020) examined self-protective behaviours and perceptions of cyber risk in a sample of 595 adults in Australia but found no significant connection was found between whether someone had previously been a victim of cybercrime and their self-protective behaviours. Drew (2020) speculated that there could be several reasons for this unexpected result, such as for example individuals not knowing how to develop self-protective cyber behaviours.

Various techniques have been proposed to mitigate the harms caused by phishing emails, including legal processes, educational initiatives (Mohammad, Thabtah, & McCluskey, 2015), and gamification techniques (Hale, Gamble, & Gamble, 2015). This latter technique of gamification – using elements of gameplay to make an activity such as employee training more fun – is an example of an attempt to encourage people to be more engaged with cybersecurity materials. Similarly, Khalid and El-Maliki (2020) demonstrated that a storytelling approach can be an effective technique for improving cybersecurity awareness and understanding. These approaches recognise that many people do not have a strong intrinsic motivation to understand cybersecurity or do appreciate that this is an important topic but struggle to read cybersecurity policies that are written in an obtuse way. Nearly every large organisation has a cybersecurity policy, yet it is difficult to imagine that these are read by most of the employees and members of that organisation.

Prevention strategies have been applied to other forms of cyber-risk. In the USA for example children aged 11 and 12 years old have been included in education campaigns about online sexual predators, which include awareness sessions that previously only parents of children and other relevant adults were invited to (Gibson, 2016). This approach uses fear appeals, such as the speaker noting that online predators refer to activities as bunny hunting. Not surprisingly, such campaigns often provoke discussion around how much information it is appropriate to give children about the risks they may experience online. Part of this relates to recognition that it is important for children and young people to learn how to use digital technologies, as these technologies are ubiquitous and an increasing part of everyday life. As such, prevention of harm through abstinence – as in no use of digital devices at all – is not feasible. Instead, a harm reduction approach is used in which children and young people are empowered to identify and protect themselves from cyber-risks. This has led to the creation of organisations and resources that seek to help parents and children in understanding cyber-risks and protective strategies, such as Internet Matters (https://www.internetmatters.org).

Prevention strategies are not limited to those who may become victims of cyber-attacks. Work can also be done to prevent individuals from becoming involved in cybercriminal activities. As discussed in Chapter 3, people who become involved in hacking often seem to do so because of their innate curiosity of computers and the internet. Whilst they may engage in criminal activities, for many this is an incidental outcome of their actions, rather than being their goal. This is not meant to diminish or excuse the harms caused by cybercriminals, and there are of course examples of cybercriminal actions that are motivated by a desire to engage with clearly illegal and amoral actions, such as the sharing of child abuse imagery. The point instead is that there may be some individuals who could be encouraged to use their skills and passions for understanding computer systems for positive uses. As discussed in Chapter 3, it has been found that hackers have differing opinions on whether gaps in cybersecurity systems should be exploited (Thackray, Richardson, Dogan, Taylor, & McAlaney, 2017), and discussions on surface hacking forums typically discourage less experienced members from engaging in illegal activities (McAlaney, Hambidge, Kimpton, & Thackray, 2020). That is, people are encouraged towards being a white hat (a hacker who works ethically and legally), and away from being a black hat (a criminal hacker) – albeit with recognition that it may be difficult for a hacker to become fully expert in hacking without some experience of activities that include an element of illegality (known as being a grey hat). In a survey of people who identify as hackers, it was found that only 9% of respondents described themselves as a black hat hacker, with the remainder describing themselves as a white hat hacker (38%), grey hat hacker (49%), or another lesser used term such as a cyberpunk (Thackray et al., 2017). There has been discussion around licensing hackers in Singapore (Wong, 2017), on the basis that providing hackers with formal recognition of their role will result in greater regulation and reduced criminality. This could though be some barriers in such an approach. It has been observed that hacker subcultures have a strong distrust of law enforcement and governments in general, in part because of past attempts to identify and prosecute hackers (T. J. Holt, 2007). Overall, hackers have been reported to perceive the criminal justice system as antagonistic and biased towards hackers, creating a sense of injustice within hacking communities (T. Holt, Brewer, & Goldsmith, 2018; T. J. Holt, Stonhouse, Freilich, & Chermak, 2021).

Prevention strategies aimed at people who would otherwise become involved in criminal hacking may also be important because such individuals do not fully understand the risks involved in hacking activities. In 2016, the then Chief Technology Officer of the National Cyber Security Centre of the UK commented that hackers are 'not as sophisticated as they think they are' (Levy, 2016), meaning that they expose themselves to risk of identification and prosecution to a far greater degree than some hackers may realise. Nevertheless there is, as discussed, a need to encourage people with an interest in computers to develop careers in this area, so as to address the cybersecurity recruitment crisis. Perhaps the approach to take is to consider educating people, particularly young adults, to approach hacking as they would any activity that can be done legally, but which can include risks. This is already done extensively throughout health and social education in schools for topics such as alcohol use and safer sex and is part of the training for regulated sports and fitness activities such as sports leagues.

Rennie and Shore (2007) argue that there are steps that could be taken to reduce engagement in criminal hacking, including:

- Interventions by parents and peers to teach young people about the criminal nature of hacking.
- Reducing the attractiveness of hacking.
- Police monitoring of signs of new hackers and early interventions in the form of warnings and behavioural contracts.
- Curtailing the availability of hacking tools, to i) create a higher entry barrier and ii) to prevent the flow experience.

These recommendations reflect elements of prevention and intervention strategies that have been used in other domains, although some caution should be applied given the unique characteristics of hacking and cybercrime. For instance, peer education (such as an awareness session delivered by an adolescent of the same age as the target group) has been found to be an effective strategy in reducing harmful behaviours in health risks in other domains (Abdi & Simbar, 2013), and the role of parental influence in adolescent health and social behaviours has also been established (Beck & Treiman, 1996). However, problems may arise when it comes to peers and parents educating the target population about the legalities of hacking, given the number of legislative grey areas and outdated laws around computing use that exist in many countries. In addition, parents may not themselves have the knowledge to speak to their children about hacking. This is something that has been targeted by the National Crime Agency in the UK, which has a campaign that aims to empower parents into having meaningful discussions with their children about hacking, including the legitimate and positive careers that exist in this area (National Crime Agency, 2023). The NCA also runs a rehab camp in which offenders, typically teenagers, are encouraged to utilise their skills for the social good (Ward, 2017).

As commented by Rennie and Shore (2007) engagement in cybercrime could also be lowered by reducing the attractiveness of criminal hacking, although this could be a challenge given media depictions of hacking that often contain glamour and excitement, such as the movie *Blackhat*, featuring Marvel star Chris Hemsworth. There are though examples of relatively more realistic depictions of hackers that more deeply explore the nuances of black, white, and grey hat hacking and the dilemmas faced by hackers, such as the television show *Mr. Robot*. It could be argued that media depictions of hacking and hackers are not in themselves an issue, provided a clear effort is made to convey the many, often highly paid, opportunities there are to have legitimate career paths in cybersecurity – including ethical hacking, and the reality of prosecution and criminal records that can result from illegal hacking. As discussed in Chapter 3, this would help address the cybersecurity recruitment crisis. Both police monitoring of new potential hackers and curtailing the availability of hacking tools would likely help prevent people from becoming involved in hacking, but the challenge with each of these is the scale of the problem and the amount of time and resources required. Law enforcement and intelligence agencies may also be reluctant to publicly comment on the ability they have to access and monitor online communications, although it has been reported that the UK intelligence agency MI5 has a Behavioural Science Institute that aims to identify individuals who may engage in terrorism (Gardner, 2016).

It has been suggested that Sykes and Matza's (1957) neutralisation theory could be applied to better understand and prevent cybercrime (Bossler, 2021). This theory aims to explain why juveniles who otherwise appear to conform to societal norms can commit acts of deviance, despite not being part of a deviant sub-culture or believing themselves to be a deviant. It states that the juveniles in question will seek to use techniques of neutralisation to justify the acceptability of their behaviour, and in doing so avoid any feeling of conflict with their overall general belief system. In other words, they try to find a way to tell themselves that they are not a bad person, despite engaging in activities that would be viewed as negative in mainstream society. Sykes and Matza (1957) identify five techniques that individuals use to achieve this neutralisation: denial of responsibility (not their fault; it occurred due to forces outside of their control); denial of injury (viewing the deviant behaviour as being victimless); denial of the victim (removing the victim's 'victimhood' status by perceiving the victim as deserving of the harm inflicted); condemnation of the condemners (attempts to shift the focus away from the offender behaviour and onto the perceived hypocrisy of the condemners); and finally appeal to higher loyalties (prioritising the needs of family and friends over following the law). There are certainly many cases where these techniques are utilised by hackers and cybercriminals. Denial of the victim is evident in cases of hacking where attackers discuss their targets as being responsible for the attack due to their lax cybersecurity, as seen in online conversations within hacking groups (G. Coleman, 2014). As previously stated, it has been observed that cybercriminals use language that dehumanises and demonises their victims (M. Rogers, 2010). Similarly, condemnation of the condemners is something that has been observed in situations where hackers are prosecuted for crimes and claim that the punishment they receive is disproportionate to the harm caused and intended, satisfying the need for revenge by the organisation they targeted (Hutchings, 2013; Knappenberger, 2012). Denial of injury has also been documented amongst hackers, with Hutchings (2013) reporting that hackers often deny that their computer intrusions have caused any harm. Finally, an appeal to high loyalties as a neutralisation technique is evident, with hackers viewing their actions as being for the greater good (Chua & Holt, 2016). Examples of this would be the hacktivist collective Anonymous providing advice to citizens in Tunisia on how to access the internet after the Tunisian Government restricted online access during the revolution of 2011 (DeTardo-Bora, Clark, & Gardner, 2019; Olson, 2012).

As Bossler (2021) notes there have been further techniques of neutralisation suggested in the literature since Sykes and Matza's (1957) initial identification of five techniques. These include the defence of necessity (because the action was necessary in a specific situation) which was identified by Minor (1981); metaphor of the ledger (one's belief that one has done more good than bad in life) as posited by Klockars (1975); and normalcy and entitlement (where individuals argue that most others engage in a similar behaviour and they deserve to be occasionally awarded), described by J. W. Coleman (1985). Finally, Cromwell and Thurman (2003) suggest justification by comparison (the offender stating that they could commit a worse crime). These neutralisation techniques could be applied to cybercrime incidents. Hacktivists frequently acknowledge that their actions are illegal, but frame these as being a necessity in addressing the unethical practices of organisations and governments (Olson, 2012). Similarly, hackers have been observed to argue that their crimes are often, by comparison, relatively minor compared to serious offline crimes (Olson, 2012). These techniques of neutralisation have been studied in relation to several cyber-deviant behaviours, including digital piracy (Popham & Volpe, 2018), sexting (Renfrow & Rollo, 2014), and hacking (Morris, 2010). Brewer, Fox, and Miller (2020) note that the evidence for the use of neutralisation techniques in cybercrime is mixed, highlighting the need for more research in this area. Looking more specifically at hacking, Hutchings (2013) reported that, in comparison to other types of cybercrime (e.g., digital piracy), hackers do not deny responsibility for their actions and instead argue that they are in control of the incident. This is consistent with work that has demonstrated that gaining prestige and demonstrating superior knowledge are important motivators for engaging with hacking communities (McAlaney et al., 2020; Seebruck, 2015). Bossler (2021) explored the role of neutralisation techniques in the willingness of college students to commit cyber-attacks, finding that these techniques were significant predictors even after controlling for peer influence, computer skills, time spent online, and gender. Within these results, there were some relationships, or lack of relationships, between specific neutralisation techniques and specific types of cybercrime. For instance, denial of injury was not significantly related with willingness to hack government services, with the governments in the examples given in the study framed as behaving in ways that were causing harm. As Bossler (2021) observes, some acts of hacking such as hacktivism are conducted with the deliberate aim of causing harm.

Research into neutralisation techniques has been used as the basis of several criminal justice innovations, such as situational crime prevention (Cornish, 2003). This approach involves several strategies, such as challenging the excuses that offenders use to justify their actions. This is intended to prompt the offender to consider their actions at the point when they are on the verge of committing a cybercrime. Bossler (2021) suggests that this can be further achieved through educating hackers on the financial and emotional consequences to individuals and organisations that can result from being hacked. This has parallels with prevention approaches that have been suggested for the potential victims of cybercrime, such as those who may be targeted by phishing emails or other social engineering attacks – ultimately the goal is to encourage the individual to think more deeply about their actions (i.e., being a naïve scientist as opposed to being a cognitive miser, as discussed in Chapter 5). In addition, another approach is making individuals explicitly aware of how they may be using neutralisation techniques to justify their behaviour to themselves. There is some precedence of this from work on how to empower individuals to challenge fake news. This involves prompting epistemic cognition in individuals, which refers to an individual's knowledge about their own knowledge (Barzilai & Zohar, 2012; Mason, Junyent, & Tornatora, 2014). In other words, if hackers can be prompted to consider why they believe in the neutralisation techniques they use to justify attacks, then they may realise that justifications are erroneous. However, caution should be taken in using such approaches with hackers. As previously noted, hacking communities are particularly resistant to attempts to change their behaviour or beliefs. As Bossler (2021) acknowledges, hacktivists in particular have a strong desire to achieve their goal, and consciously wish to cause harm to their targets.

More broadly, Chung, Chen, Chang, and Chou (2006) make four recommendations to combat cybercrime – i) regularly update existing laws; ii) enhance specialised task forces; iii) use civil resources; and iv) promote cybersecurity research. The first point is one that certainly needs to be addressed. As has been commented elsewhere, legislation around cyber behaviours is frequently outdated and not fit for purpose (Halder, 2022). However, it is also acknowledged that there is a challenge in keeping legislation up to date when technologies can evolve so quickly. This suggests the need for more flexible legislation that can be adapted to new technologies and methods of online crime. At the time of writing, the United Nations are holding an ad hoc committee to develop an international convention on countering the use of information and communication technologies for criminal purposes (United Nations Office on Drug and Crime, 2023). Specialist task forces could also be beneficial, given the unique characteristics of cybercrime, as suggested by An and Kim (2018). For example, the complexity of the cybercrime ecosystem could pose a barrier to investigation for the law enforcement agents who are not familiar with cybercrime. In support of this, An and Kim (2018) argue that greater classification and definition of CaaS will enable governments to improve national defence and security, by shaping roles and the adoption of regulatory practices. Greater collaboration between governments, law enforcement agencies, security providers and software vendors will also aide prevention and intervention strategies (Chung et al., 2006). It has been noted that this type of collaboration may be especially beneficial for addressing immediate cyber-threats in risky situations (Majchrzak & Jarvenpaa, 2010).

It has been noted that there has been a growth of a 'new' private security industry and private policing industries in cyberspace (Button, 2020). As the author notes, this has parallels to the 'quiet revolution' that occurred in the 1970s and 1980s in private security in North America, which was prompted in part by under-funding of the police. Many online spaces are regulated by the companies who provide online services, such as social media platforms or gaming. This can involve partnerships with the police for criminal investigations. There is though a lack of preventative policing. Within large organisations the cybersecurity is typically the responsibility of what is called the Chief Information Security Officer (CISO). Facebook has a Community Operations Team who investigate complaints and moderate content, although concerns have been raised about the workload and mental health of those who are employed in this role (Newton, 2019). Several large companies are known for providing cybersecurity services, such as PWC, BAE, IBM, Symantec, RSA and Kapersky, as well as smaller companies that cater to smaller firms, and specialist companies such as Bulletproof that offer penetration services (Button, 2020). Prevention and investigation are also increasingly undertaken by the voluntary section, such as through websites that provide people with the opportunity to watch CCTV and report potential incidents (Button, 2020). More proactive voluntary groups take on forms of online vigilantism, such as on www.419eater.com, where attempts are made to engage with scammers to waste their time and prevent them from scamming a real victim. One of the more extreme xamplees of these vigilante groups are what have been termed paedophile hunters, who are groups who pose as children online with the aim of exposing paedophiles who attempt to engage them in sexual activity. Videos of the alleged paedophile being confronted by group members are popular on social media platforms, with it being reported in 2018 that there were over 75 such groups active in the UK alone (Evans, 2018). Button (2020) observes that there is a lack of understanding and regulation of this new private security system. It has also been argued that the continued existence of cybercriminal firms in some countries is due to a lack of police efforts against cybercrime (Lusthaus, Kleemans, Leukfeldt, Levi, & Holt, 2023).

References

Abdi, F., & Simbar, M. (2013). The Peer Education Approach in Adolescents- Narrative Review Article. *Iran J Public Health, 42*(11), 1200–1206.

Adams, A. T., Costa, J., Jung, M. F., & Choudhury, T. (2015). *Mindless computing: designing technologies to subtly influence behavior.* Paper presented at the Proceedings of the 2015 ACM International Joint Conference on Pervasive and Ubiquitous Computing, Osaka, Japan. https://doi.org/10.1145/2750858.2805843

Ajzen, I. (1991). The theory of planned behaviour. *Organizational Behavior and Human Decision Processes, 50*, 179–211.

Ajzen, I., & Fishbein, M. (1980). *Understanding Attitudes and Predicting Social Behaviour.* Englewood Cliffs, N.J.: Prentice Hall.

An, J., & Kim, H.-W. (2018). A Data Analytics Approach to the Cybercrime Underground Economy. *IEEE Access, 6.* doi:10.1109/ACCESS.2018.2831667

Bada, M., & Nurse, J. (2019). Developing cybersecurity education and awareness programmes for small- and medium-sized enterprises (SMEs). *Information and Computer Security.* doi:10.1108/ICS-07–2018–0080

Bada, M., Sasse, A., & Nurse, J. (2015). *Cyber security awareness campaigns: Why do they fail to change behaviour?* Paper presented at the International Conference on Cyber Security for Sustainable Society, Coventry, UK.

Bandura, A. (2003). Social cognitive theory. In Ewen, R. B. (Ed.), *An Introduction to the Theories of Personality* (pp. 365–386). Mahwa: Lawrence Erlbraun Associates.

Barzilai, S., & Zohar, A. (2012). Epistemic Thinking in Action: Evaluating and Integrating Online Sources. *Cognition and Instruction, 30*(1), 39–85. doi:10.1080/07370008.2011.636495

Beck, K. H., & Treiman, K. A. (1996). The relationship of social context of drinking, perceived social norms, and parental influence to various drinking patterns of adolescents. *Addictive Behaviors, 21*(5), 633–644. doi:10.1016/0306-4603(95)00087-9

Bossler, A. M. (2021). Neutralizing Cyber Attacks: Techniques of Neutralization and Willingness to Commit Cyber Attacks. *American Journal of Criminal Justice, 46*(6), 911–934. doi:10.1007/s12103-021-09654-5

Brewer, R., Fox, S., & Miller, C. (2020). Applying the Techniques of Neutralization to the Study of Cybercrime. In Holt, T. J., and Bossler, A. M. (Eds) *The Palgrave Handbook of International Cybercrime and Cyberdeviance*. Cham: Palgrave Macmillan (pp. 1–19).

Button, M. (2020). The "New" Private Security Industry, the Private Policing of Cyberspace and the Regulatory Questions. *Journal of Contemporary Criminal Justice, 36*(1), 39–55. doi:10.1177/1043986219890194

Caraban, A., Karapanos, E., Gonçalves, D., & Campos, P. (2019). *23 Ways to Nudge: A Review of Technology-Mediated Nudging in Human-Computer Interaction*. Paper presented at the Proceedings of the 2019 CHI Conference on Human Factors in Computing Systems, Glasgow, Scotland. https://doi.org/10.1145/3290605.3300733

Chua, Y. T., & Holt, T. (2016). A Cross-National Examination of the Techniques of Neutralization to Account for Hacking Behaviors. *Victims & Offenders, 11*, 1–22. doi:10.1080/15564886.2015.1121944

Chung, W., Chen, H.-c., Chang, W., & Chou, S. (2006). Fighting cybercrime: A review and the Taiwan experience. *Decision Support Systems, 41*, 669–682. doi:10.1016/j.dss.2004.06.006

Cohen, L. E., & Felson, M. (1979). Social Change and Crime Rate Trends: A Routine Activity Approach. *American Sociological Review, 44*(4), 588–608. doi:10.2307/2094589

Coleman, G. (2014). *Hacker, Hoaxer, Whistleblower, Spy: The Many Faces Of Anonymous*. London: Verso.

Coleman, J. W. (1985). *The criminal elite: The sociology of white collar crime*. London: St. Martin's Press.

Cornish, D. (2003). Opportunities, Precipitators, and Criminal Decisions: A Reply to Wortley's Critique of Situational Crime Prevention. *Crime Prevention Studies, 16*, 41–96.

Cromwell, P., & Thurman, Q. (2003). The devil made me do it: use of neutralizations by shoplifters. *Deviant Behavior, 24*(6), 535–550. doi:10.1080/713840271

Davis, R., Campbell, R., Hildon, Z., Hobbs, L., & Michie, S. (2015). Theories of behaviour and behaviour change across the social and behavioural sciences: a scoping review. *Health Psychology Review, 9*(3), 323–344. doi:10.1080/17437199.2014.941722

DeTardo-Bora, K., Clark, E., & Gardner, B. (2019). "I Did What I Believe Is Right": A Study of Neutralizations among Anonymous Operation Participants. *Journal of Qualitative Criminal Justice & Criminology*. doi:10.21428/88de04a1.5c02a7d3

Drew, J. M. (2020). A study of cybercrime victimisation and prevention: exploring the use of online crime prevention behaviours and strategies. *Journal of Criminological Research, Policy and Practice, 6*(1), 17–33. doi:10.1108/JCRPP-12-2019-0070

Evans, M. (2018). Paedophile hunters like a 'cottage industry', court hears as three groups target same suspect. Retrieved from https://www.telegraph.co.uk/news/2018/01/09/paedophile-hunters-now-operating-like-cottage-industry-court/

Fagbule, O. (2023). *Cyber Security Training in Small to Medium-sized Enterprises (SMEs): Exploring Organisation Culture and Employee Training Needs*. PhD, Bournemouth University,

Fisher, J. D., & Fisher, W. A. (1996). The Information-Motivation-Behavioral skills model of AIDS risk behavior change: Empirical support and application. In *Understanding and preventing HIV risk behavior: Safer sex and drug use*. Thousand Oaks, CA, US: Sage Publications, Inc. (pp. 100–127).

Gardner, F. (2016). How MI5's scientists work to identify future terrorists. Retrieved from https://www.bbc.co.uk/news/uk-38252470

Gibson, C. (2016). 'They call it bunny hunting'. Retrieved from https://www.washingtonpost.com/lifestyle/style/they-call-it-bunny-hunting-how-authorities-warn-kids-about-online-predators/2016/09/06/2044ee40-5980-11e6-9767-f6c947fd0cb8_story.html

Gutek, B. A., & Winter, S. J. (1990). Computer use, control over computers, and job-satisfaction. *People's Reactions to Technology, 4*, 121–144. Retrieved from://WOS:A1990BT40C00004

Hadnagy, C. (2018). *Social Engineering: The Science of Human Hacking*. Indianapolis, IN: Wiley.

Halder, D. (2022). *Cyber victimology: decoding cyber crime victimization*. New York: Routledge.

Hale, M. L., Gamble, R. F., & Gamble, P. (2015). *CyberPhishing: A Game-Based Platform for Phishing Awareness Testing*. Paper presented at the 2015 48th Hawaii International Conference on System Sciences, 5–8 Jan.

Harbach, M., Hettig, M., Weber, S., & Smith, M. (2014). *Using personal examples to improve risk communication for security & privacy decisions*. Paper presented at the Proceedings of the SIGCHI Conference on Human Factors in Computing Systems, Toronto, Ontario, Canada. https://doi.org/10.1145/2556288.2556978

Hesseling, R. B. P. (2006). *Displacement: A review of the empirical literature*. Research and Documentation Centre, Ministry of Justice, The Netherlands.

Holt, T., Brewer, R., & Goldsmith, A. (2018). Digital Drift and the "Sense of Injustice": Counter-Productive Policing of Youth Cybercrime. *Deviant Behavior, 40*. doi:10.1080/01639625.2018.1472927

Holt, T. J. (2007). Subcultural evolution? examining the influence of on- and off-line experiences on deviant subcultures. *Deviant Behavior, 28*(2), 171–198. doi:10.1080/01639620601131065

Holt, T. J., Stonhouse, M., Freilich, J., & Chermak, S. M. (2021). Examining Ideologically Motivated Cyberattacks Performed by Far-Left Groups. *Terrorism and Political Violence, 33*(3), 527–548. doi:10.1080/09546553.2018.1551213

Hutchings, A. (2013). Hacking and Fraud: Qualitative Analysis of Online Offending and Victimization. In Jaishankar, K., and Ronel, N. (Eds). *Global Criminology: Crime and Victimization in a Globalized Era*. New York: Routledge (pp. 93–114).

Iuga, C., Nurse, J. R. C., & Erola, A. (2016). Baiting the hook: factors impacting susceptibility to phishing attacks. *Human-centric Computing and Information Sciences, 6*(1), 8. doi:10.1186/s13673-016-0065-2

Johnston, A. C., Warkentin, M., & Siponen, M. (2015). An enhanced fear appeal rhetorical framework: Leveraging threats to the human asset through sanctioning rhetoric. *MIS Quarterly, 39*(1), 113–134. Retrieved from://WOS:000348600600007

Khalid, F., & El-Maliki, T. (2020). Teachers' experiences in the development of digital storytelling for cyber risk awareness. *International Journal of Advanced Computer Science and Applications, 11*(2), 186–191. Retrieved from://WOS:000518468600025

Kioskli, K., Fotis, T., Nifakos, S., & Mouratidis, H. (2023). The Importance of Conceptualising the Human-Centric Approach in Maintaining and Promoting Cybersecurity-Hygiene in Healthcare 4.0. *Applied Sciences-Basel, 13*(6). doi:10.3390/app13063410

Klockars, C. B. (1975). *The professional fence*. London: Tavistock Publications.

Knappenberger, B. (Writer & Director). (2012). *We Are Legion: The Story of the Hacktivists*. Netflix.

Konstantinou, L., Caraban, A. K., & Karapanos, E. (2019). *Combating Misinformation Through Nudging*. Paper presented at the IFIP TC13 International Conference on Human-Computer Interaction.

Lee, M. K., Kiesler, S., & Forlizzi, J. (2011). *Mining behavioral economics to design persuasive technology for healthy choices*. Paper presented at the Proceedings of the SIGCHI

Conference on Human Factors in Computing Systems, Vancouver, BC, Canada. https://doi.org/10.1145/1978942.1978989

Levy, I. (2016). Hackers are 'not as sophisticated as they think they are'. Retrieved from https://www.wired.co.uk/article/ian-levy-national-centre-cyber-security

Lusthaus, J., Kleemans, E., Leukfeldt, R., Levi, M., & Holt, T. (2023). Cybercriminal networks in the UK and Beyond: Network structure, criminal cooperation and external interactions. *Trends in Organized Crime.* doi:10.1007/s12117-022-09476-9

Majchrzak, A. N. N., & Jarvenpaa, S. L. (2010). Safe Contexts for Interorganizational Collaborations Among Homeland Security Professionals. *Journal of Management Information Systems, 27*(2), 55–86. Retrieved from http://www.jstor.org/stable/29780171

Mason, L., Junyent, A. A., & Tornatora, M. C. (2014). Epistemic evaluation and comprehension of web-source information on controversial science-related topics: Effects of a short-term instructional intervention. *Computers & Education, 76*(Supplement C), 143–157. doi:https://doi.org/10.1016/j.compedu.2014.03.016

McAlaney, J., Hambidge, S., Kimpton, E., & Thackray, H. (2020). *Knowledge is power: An analysis of discussions on hacking forums.* Paper presented at the 2020 IEEE European Symposium on Security and Privacy Workshops (EuroS&PW), 7–11 Sept.

Michie, S., van Stralen, M. M., & West, R. (2011). The behaviour change wheel: A new method for characterising and designing behaviour change interventions. *Implementation Science, 6*(1), 42. doi:10.1186/1748-5908-6-42

Minor, W. W. (1981). Techniques of Neutralization: a Reconceptualization and Empirical Examination. *Journal of Research in Crime and Delinquency, 18*(2), 295–318. doi:10.1177/002242788101800206

Mohammad, R. M., Thabtah, F., & McCluskey, L. (2015). Tutorial and critical analysis of phishing websites methods. *Computer Science Review, 17,* 1–24. doi:https://doi.org/10.1016/j.cosrev.2015.04.001

Montoya, L., Junger, M., & Ongena, Y. (2016). The Relation Between Residential Property and Its Surroundings and Day- and Night-Time Residential Burglary. *Environment and Behavior, 48*(4), 515–549. doi:10.1177/0013916514551047

Morris, R. (2010). Computer Hacking and the Techniques of Neutralization: An Empirical Assessment. *Corporate Hacking and Technology-Driven Crime: Social Dynamics and Implications.* doi:10.4018/978-1-61692-805-6.ch001

National Crime Agency. (2023). *HACKING IT LEGAL: Help your child to make positive choices.* Retrieved from https://www.nationalcrimeagency.gov.uk/who-we-are/publications/525-cyber-choices-hacking-it-legal-parents-guardians-carers/file

Ncubukezi, T., Mwansa, L., & Rocaries, F. (2020). A Review of the Current Cyber Hygiene in Small and Medium-sized Businesses. *2020 15th International Conference for Internet Technology and Secured Transactions (ICITST),* London, United Kingdom, pp. 1–6, doi: 10.23919/ICITST51030.2020.9351339

Newton, C. (2019). The trauma floor: The scret lives of Facebook moderators in America. Retrieved from https://www.theverge.com/2019/2/25/18229714/cognizant-facebook-content-moderator-interviews-trauma-working-conditions-arizona

Olson, P. (2012). *We Are Anonymous.* New York: Back Bay Books.

Popham, J. F., & Volpe, C. (2018). *Predicting Moral Disengagement from the Harms Associated with Digital Music Piracy: An Exploratory, Integrative Test of Digital Drift and the Criminal Interaction Order.*

Prochaska, J. O., Johnson, S., & Lee, P. (2009). The Transtheoretical Model of behavior change. In *The handbook of health behavior change, 3rd ed.* (pp. 59–83). New York: Springer Publishing Company.

Radcliffe, J. (2023). *People Hacker: Confessions of a Burglar for Hire*. London: Simon & Schuster.

Renfrow, D. G., & Rollo, E. A. (2014). Sexting on Campus: Minimizing Perceived Risks and Neutralizing Behaviors. *Deviant Behavior, 35*(11), 903–920. doi:10.1080/01639625.2014.897122

Rennie, L., & Shore, M. (2007). An Advanced Model of Hacking. *Security Journal, 20*(4), 236–251. doi:10.1057/palgrave.sj.8350019

Rhysider, J. (2022). ZeuS. *Darknet Diaries*. Retrieved from https://darknetdiaries.com/episode/111/

Rogers, M. (2010). The Psyche of Cybercriminals: A Psycho-Social Perspective. In Ghosh, S., and Turini, E. (Eds), *Cybercrimes: A Multidisciplinary Analysis* (pp. 217–235). Heidelberg: Springer Berlin.

Rogers, R. W. (1975). A Protection Motivation Theory of Fear Appeals and Attitude Change. *J Psychol, 91*(1), 93–114. doi:10.1080/00223980.1975.9915803

Seebruck, R. (2015). A typology of hackers: Classifying cyber malfeasance using a weighted arc circumplex model. *Digital Investigation, 14*, 36–45. doi:http://dx.doi.org/10.1016/j.diin.2015.07.002

Steindl, C., Jonas, E., Sittenthaler, S., Traut-Mattausch, E., & Greenberg, J. (2015). Understanding psychological reactance: New developments and findings. *Zeitschrift fur Psychologie, 223*(4), 205–214. doi:10.1027/2151-2604/a000222

Sykes, G. M., & Matza, D. (1957). Techniques of Neutralization: A Theory of Delinquency. *American Sociological Review, 22*(6), 664–670. doi:10.2307/2089195

Taylor-Jackson, J., McAlaney, J., Foster, J. L., Bello, A., Maurushat, A., & Dale, J. (2020). *Incorporating Psychology into Cyber Security Education: A Pedagogical Approach*. Paper presented at the Financial Cryptography and Data Security Conference, Cham.

Taylor, J., McAlaney, J., Hodge, S., Thackray, H., Richardson, C., James, S., & Dale, J. (2017). *Teaching psychological principles to cybersecurity students*. Paper presented at the 2017 IEEE Global Engineering Education Conference (EDUCON), 25–28 April.

Thackray, H., Richardson, C., Dogan, H., Taylor, J., & McAlaney, J. (2017). *Surveying the hackers: The challenges of data collection from a secluded community*. Paper presented at the 16th European Conference on Cyber Warfare and Security, Dublin.

Thaler, R. H., & Sunstein, C. R. (2009). *Nudge: Improving Decisions About Health, Wealth and Happiness*. London: Penguin.

United Nations Office on Drug and Crime. (2023). Ad Hoc Committee to Elaborate a Comprehensive International Convention on Countering the Use of Information and Communications Technologies for Criminal Purposes. Retrieved from https://www.unodc.org/unodc/en/cybercrime/ad_hoc_committee/home

Ward, M. (2017). Rehab camp aims to put young cyber-crooks on right track. Retrieved from https://www.bbc.co.uk/news/technology-40629887

Williams, K. (2012). Fear Appeal Theory. *Research in Business and Economics Journal, 5*, 63–82.

Wong, J. I. (2017). The country with the world's best cybersecurity is planning a new law to license hackers. Retrieved from https://qz.com/1026300/singapores-government-wants-to-license-hackers

Zimmermann, V., & Renaud, K. (2019). Moving from a 'human-as-problem' to a 'human-as-solution' cybersecurity mindset. *International Journal of Human-Computer Studies, 131*, 169–187. doi:10.1016/j.ijhcs.2019.05.005

Emergent technologies and future directions

7

Context

As discussed throughout this book, an ongoing challenge in cybersecurity is that technology continues to evolve and change. At times this can seem to happen very rapidly, such the sharp rise in prominence of artificial intelligence (AI) in 2023 (Heilweil, 2023). As will be explored in this chapter however, opportunities can also be provided by such technological advances.

Eye tracking

One example of how technology could be used to enhance cybersecurity is eye-tracking. Eye movements can reveal a great deal of information about the cognitive state of an individual, what they are looking at (endogenous cueing), what attracts attention (exogenous cueing), and the interaction between these components. While there is no one-to-one mapping between where someone is looking and their attention, the correlation between what one is looking at and the intention to process it is very high, especially for reading. Different eye movement metrics measure different aspects of cognitive and/ or emotional processing (Nam, Hong, Chung, & Noh, 2022). 'Dwell time' measures how long a participant focuses on a particular point and typically indicates its importance to the current task. 'Fixation count' is the number of times a particular part of a stimulus is looked at. The more fixations, the more active processing is engaged in. However, the longer the individual fixation (glance duration), the more holistic the processing. When a participant looks at an area, then looks away, then

DOI: 10.4324/9781003300359-7

returns to it (a regression), this suggests (Guo, 2012) that it was not fully processed the first time and requires re-encoding – potentially due to the novelty, surprising nature of the stimulus, or the difficulty which processing entails. Saccade length (quick eye movement between two or more fixation points) is known to be affected by participants' internal states, such that those under more stress have shorter saccades (Nam et al., 2022), or processing less predictable information (Liu, Tong, & Su, 2020). Indeed, predictability of eye movement patterns measured through Markov chain models can be used to establish how well someone knows how to code a stimulus, which provides insight into how that person has perceived and processed the information presented to them (Shang, Lu, Wu, & Wei, 2021). Further, eye movement differences can be used to classify depressed people from non-depressed people (Zhang et al., 2022) and those more at risk of simulated driving accidents than others (Li, Fan, Ren, Zheng, & Yang, 2021).

Traditionally, eye tracking has been done using laboratory-based eye tracking equipment. Such equipment is highly accurate; however, these eye trackers require the participant to sit in a fixed position in front of a screen, often entailing a visit to a specialist site. More recently, there has been a move towards conducting eye tracking through laptop and PC webcams, or smartphone cameras. This is an emergent technology that utilises the higher resolution available in modern web cameras to conduct eye tracking within an individual's home or workplace; in doing so it potentially creates a more naturalistic setting. This is highly relevant to cybersecurity, where it has been demonstrated that cybersecurity behaviours such as engagement with phishing emails is dependent on the social environment in which a person is placed (da Veiga, Astakhova, Botha, & Herselman, 2020). As such there is potential for webcam-based eye tracking to be used to better understand how individuals engage with phishing emails. However, the research on this topic to date has several limitations. There is a lack of research that has explored the use of webcam-based eye tracking application in relation to phishing emails on smartphones. In addition, there is a lack of research that has compared the efficacy of webcam-based eye tracking on laptops/ PCs/ smartphones against lab-based eye tracking equipment. The research that has been done has typically used relatively small sample sizes of less than 50 people, which limits the generalisability of the findings. Finally, research has often been from a computing perspective, lacking the interdisciplinary insights that can be obtained by including psychological theories.

Big data, machine learning, and artificial intelligence

Big data refers to data that is so extensive that it cannot be stored, processed, shared, and analysed by conventional means and in a reasonable timescale.

This is however somewhat context dependent. A 50mb file for example may not be a particularly large file in light of the amount of data people use on a daily basis, yet many email systems will still not permit a file of that size to be attached. Often though big data is used to refer to data that is very vast, typically generated by activities individuals engage in which generate data. For example, the collective data from all the fitness tracking devices used in a population provides a large amount of information which could potentially provide researchers and healthcare providers with insights into health behaviours that would be very difficult to collect in traditional ways. Another common source of big data is how employees with a company engage with their own IT systems. This can include a multitude of different types of information, such as the times that employees are active on the system, the emails and messages they send, the functions they perform, and how their productivity varies throughout the day. For cybersecurity, this data could include metrics such as the time between an email being opened and responded to, whether employees are attempting to access files they should not be, and if there are patterns of certain employees clicking on phishing links more than others. One form of big data is that generated by social media. As was discussed in Chapters 1, 2, and 3, social media information provides many opportunities for cybersecurity and cyberwarfare attacks, such as the use of social media bots to spread fake news. Nurse, Erola, Gibson-Robinson, Goldsmith, and Creese (2016) explored whether it is possible to separate real people from fake accounts by looking at the consistency of information provided by that person across different platforms. They found that this was indeed possible, demonstrating there are limits to how human software bots can appear to be. Adjerid and Kelley (2018) note however that psychologists have not taken full advantage of the benefits offered by big data and machine learning, in part because of the uncertainty and perceived risks around engaging with these technologies. They also argue that the increasing availability of open-source research tools means it is easier than most psychologists realise to use big data and machine learning, and that there is also a greater diversity of opportunities for using these technologies than tends to be appreciated.

Landers, Brusso, Cavanaugh, and Collmus (2016) argue big data has several advantages to data collected through more traditional means. Firstly, the data is primarily behavioural, instead of self-report data from surveys and questionnaires. This is something that may be especially beneficial when looking at cyber behaviours. Many of these behaviours are things which individuals know they either should be doing (e.g., having complex passwords) or not doing (e.g., clicking on links before properly checking the sender address). As such, self-report measures may not always be entirely reliable, particularly in the case of employees being questioned by their organisation. Secondly, the sample size that can be obtained from big data sources is substantially larger than that which can typically be achieved through traditional data collection means. Recruiting a sufficient sample to understand a phenomenon, whether for academic research or for internal research for an organisation, is a frequent challenge. Even when individuals are motivated to provide data, they may not have the time to be fully engaged with the data collection process. As big data is typically composed of information that has already been collected, such as computer records of employee behaviour within an organisation, no additional action on the part of the individual tends to be required. As such it is also attractive due to potentially using less time and fewer additional resources, instead merely using secondary data which is already there. Thirdly, the people from whom the data is being collected are not aware of this, and as a consequence issues such as demand characteristics are reduced. The concept of demand characteristics comes from research studies and refers to participants being aware of what a researcher is investigating or expects to find. This can lead to the participant doing what they think they should (e.g., saying they would not click on an unknown email when in reality they may) or acting in a way that they think will please the researcher (Orne, 1962). Alternatively the participant may respond in a way that is counter to what they perceive the researcher to want, a phenomenon identified by Masling (1966) as the 'screw you' effect. Although these processes have primarily been studied in relation to participation in academic research studies, it is possible to see how they may also arise when individuals are surveyed about their cybersecurity beliefs and behaviours. Fourthly, data can be collected at a speed that would not normally be possible. In many cases, the data may already exist. For instance, if there is a desire to explore whether a piece of fake news is spreading on social media then it is often possible to access this data immediately through software tools that can access the data from social media platforms. Finally, collection of big data is possible in populations where there may otherwise be logistical and practical challenges, such as in rural areas. Collecting data in-person from the population of a rural area could for example be time consuming and expensive, but – providing the population has online connectivity – online data can be collected quickly.

Data mining refers to the process of sorting through big data to identify patterns and relationships. Whilst this is primarily a human led activity, it draws upon techniques developed in machine learning, which is described in more detail below. Data mining has been used for prevention and intervention strategies in cybersecurity. Bartoletti, Pes, and Serusi (2018) demonstrated how data mining can be used for detecting Bitcoin addresses connected to Ponzi schemes. A Ponzi scheme is a form of investment fraud where existing investors are paid with funds collected from new investors. This illusion of being a successful, sustainable business can only be maintained whilst new investors can be found, which is naturally something that eventually is likely to come to an end. Bitcoin-based Ponzi schemes operate on the same process, by offering investors the opportunity to make a high-yield investment. The vast majority of those who invest do not however ever make any profit, nor do they get their initial investment refunded. Bitcoin-based Ponzi schemes have been found to be prolific amongst users of cryptocurrency (Vasek & Moore, 2018), despite the awareness of such scams in cryptocurrency communities (Bartoletti et al., 2018). The fact that Bartoletti et al. (2018) were able to demonstrate how Bitcoin addresses can be matched to Ponzi scams highlights one of the characteristics of the blockchain on which cryptocurrency is based – it may, on the surface, appear to enable greater anonymity, but it also means every transaction is recorded and visible.

Big data is linked to machine learning. Machine learning is when a machine has the capability to learn from previous experience, as opposed to repeating set functions regardless of the outcome. There have been several high-profile examples of machine learning in the media, such as the robots built by Boston Dynamics, who teach themselves to walk through trial and error, much the same as a human infant would (Browning, 2023). Big data can be used in conjunction with machine learning by providing existing data sets to train the machine, such as for example training a machine to post on social media in the style of a human by training it on existing posts from social media platforms. Such cases can however have unintended consequences. For example, an AI developed by Microsoft was deployed on Twitter and, learning from the responses it received, went from posting 'can I just say that im stoked to meet u? humans are super cool' [sic] to 'I fucking hate feminists and they should all die and burn in hell' and finally 'Hitler was right I hate the jews'. This all occurred within 24 hours, demonstrating the speed with which machine learning can take place is not always a positive. This example was possibly a case of unsupervised learning, in which the system is given no starting point and learns entirely through observations and interactions. Another example would be a self-driving car that is given no prior information about the rules of the road and learns them through the observation of the behaviour of other vehicles. Supervised learning on the other hand would involve the self-driving car being programmed with information relevant to the task, such as the meaning of road signs, traffic lights, and so on. Reinforcement learning can contain elements of both supervised and unsupervised learning and could for instance involve a human driver taking action to correct the car when it attempts to do something it should not. The car then learns from that experience and, ideally, should not repeat the same error again.

One positive argument that could be made for the use of machine learning is that it produces objective and rational decisions. If this is the case, then it would address one of the fundamental challenges in cybersecurity – the tendency of humans to make use of cognitive biases and heuristics when navigating our world, as discussed in Chapter 2. This can lead to what may be seen as irrational behaviour and is partly the source of the view of humans as being the weak link in cybersecurity. However, Lima and Keegan (2020) note that the supervised approach *is* often used within cybersecurity, which means that the starting point for the system is human knowledge and judgement. As such the same biases that are evident in human beliefs and decision-making may also therefore be transferred into machine learning. Big data and machine learning can also be used to quickly identify patterns it may otherwise be difficult to detect. For example, Jones, Wojcik, Sweeting, and Silver (2016) demonstrated an increase in negative emotions in Twitter communications following a mass shooting event offline. This could be used to inform prevention approaches by alerting law enforcement agencies to the possibility of an incident occurring before, and to direct resources toward monitoring for any other indications of criminal intent. Similarly, big data coupled with machine learning has also been used to predict future behaviour, including offline criminal behaviour (Benbouzid, 2019) such as where and when a crime is likely to occur. Again, this is something that could in theory be achieved by humans but would be very resource intensive to achieve on a large scale. Such predictions do of course raise ethical and legal questions about how much action should be taken against individuals who are predicted to – but have not actually committed – a criminal offence. Not surprisingly the science fiction film *Minority Report* is often cited in discussions on this topic, depicting as it does a world where individuals are arrested based on precognition that predicts they will commit a crime in future. One of the plot points in the film is that this system is open to manipulation and error. Attempting to circumvent any type of predictive system of crime is something that it would seem would be very attractive to hackers, given their level of curiosity and interest in testing the limits of systems, as discussed in Chapter 3. In support of this, Das, Baki, Aassal, Verma, and Dunbar (2020) identify several challenges in applying data science methods to detect phishing and spear-phishing attacks. This includes the fact that attackers are actively seeking ways to circumvent the security of an organisation, which includes developing new attack techniques that machine learning may not recognise. In addition, attacks can happen very quickly, which requires real-time detection and intervention.

The next step beyond machine learning is artificial intelligence (AI), although the distinction between these two concepts is quite blurred. AI has been defined by Norman (2017) as a machine or software that produces intelligent behaviour including control, planning, scheduling, diagnosis, recognition, learning, and adaptation. An aspect of AI that people may be familiar with is the concept of the Turing test, famously proposed by Alan Turing (Turing, 1950). There are different variations of this test, but ultimately it is about whether an AI can convince a human that it is another human. Early attempts to have machines converse with humans in a naturalistic way in an attempt to pass the

Turing test include ELIZA, a chatbot created at MIT between 1964 and 1966 (Agassi & Wiezenbaum, 1976). ELIZA conversed with users though a text screen, and aimed to give an illusion of understanding, although in reality the responses of the program were pre-set, depending on the various rules the program operated on. Since then, and especially in recent years, there have been substantial increases in machine learning and AI. In 2018 Google showcased its voice-based AI assistant, demonstrating how it could be used to call a hair salon, have a conversation with the employee there, and book a haircut – all apparently with the hair salon employee at the end of the phone not realising they were speaking to a machine, which could be considered to be a successful pass of the Turing test (Kastrenakes, 2020). Such examples stimulate the debate on whether AI will ever develop sentience, with some claiming this has already occurred (De Cosmo, 2022). Such questions are important, but the challenging discussion around sentience of AIs and how – or if – this can ever be proven is outside the scope of this publication. Nevertheless, there are some interesting applications of machine learning and AI to cybersecurity.

Dutta, Joyce, and Brewer (2018) explored how chatbots may be used to help cybersecurity practitioners make decisions, such as how to respond to incidents. The rationale behind this is that a cyber incident can be a high-pressure situation, in which the cybersecurity professional must process and act upon a lot of information in a short period of time. Attackers often try to push the target to move towards making quick, impulsive decisions (cognitive miser) as opposed to carefully thinking about all the information available and making a rational decision (naïve scientist). As such a chatbot can create some friction in the decision-making process and help the cybersecurity professional to distinguish the key points from the noise and make an appropriate decision. The benefits of AI are not limited to cybersecurity professionals. It has been suggested for example that AI software such as ChatGPT may 'democratize' cybercrime by undertaking the technical aspects of some hacking, thereby reducing barriers to participation (Muncaster, 2022). As discussed throughout this book, hacking is not itself a criminal activity. Nevertheless, it is reasonable to be concerned about how AI tools may enable those with criminal intent, and how they may result in those without criminal intent unintentionally becoming involved in illegal hacking activities without a full understanding of what they are doing. In addition, AI can be used to create deepfakes. These are AI generated images and videos that are fake, but which visually appear to be highly realistic. Some of the more well known examples of deepfake videos include a clip of former US President Barak Obama describing Donald Trump as a 'total dipshit', or Jon Snow from the television series *Game of Thrones* apologising to fans for what was seen to be a poor end to the show (Sample, 2020). In *Trust No One: Inside the World of Deepfakes*, Grothaus (2021) highlights the risk caused by deepfakes, outlining a world where it is increasingly difficult for people to separate fiction from reality. There is undoubtedly great potential for cyber adversaries to use deepfakes for a range of activities, including fake news, the generation of phishing emails and – by making use of technologies such as voice based chatbots – even other forms of social engineering that have until now required a human attacker. These issues have led researchers such as Guitton (2020) to identify AI as an emergent and potentially major cybersecurity risk.

Specific examples have been identified that demonstrate how machine learning and AI can be used by attackers. Baki, Verma, Mukherjee, and Gnawali (2017) for example examined the role of these technologies in email masquerade. This refers to the situation where an adversary gains access to an email account (such as for example the incident involving Anonymous and HBGary, as discussed in Chapter 3), and then uses the emails within that account to learn the writing style of the person that account belongs to. The adversary can also gain information about the contacts the target has, and the context in which previous conversations have taken place. This enables the attacker to send out new emails in which they masquerade as the target, for a range of purposes including miscommunication, causing disruption and disharmony, sending phishing emails, and spreading malware. This attack can be conducted entirely through human effort, but it is a task that could potentially be undertaken on a far greater scale by AI. In other words, AI may be able to scan all the emails and other available electronic communications (such as social media posts) by a target and quickly be able to generate a fake email that is written in the style of the target. Baki et al. (2017) tested masquerade emails and found that participants performed close to random in their ability to distinguish between real and fake masquerade emails. Research such as this highlights the evolving challenges that individuals and organisations face when attempting to safely navigate computer systems. Coupled with other AI enabled technologies such as deepfakes, attackers have increasing tools at their disposal with which to fool their targets.

Big data, machine learning and AI have also been used to understand and locate hackers. As Lima and Keegan (2020) note there is a lot of text generated on online hacking forums and social media accounts, as well as the sharing of hacking tools and information about security gaps that have been discovered. This is a greater amount of data than any human could realistically be expected to monitor and review in a realistic way within the often very short window in which to prevent an attack. In addition, big data and machine learning approaches could, in theory, be used to identify which individuals or groups are planning an attack. Further, the approach can be used to better understand the group structures and processes within hacking groups. This was attempted by Lippmann et al. (2016) in their study of social media and Reddit posts. Their analysis supports earlier research by Benjamin, Zhang, Nunamaker, and Chen (2016) who argued that there tends to be leaders and influential individuals within hacking communities. This is in contrast to what hacking groups themselves claim – such groups will often say that they have no leaders (Olson, 2012). More recently, Marin, Shakarian, & Shakarian (2018) demonstrated that machine learning could be used to identify key hackers on dark web forums. However, Lima and Keegan (2020) note several challenges in using big data and machine learning to identify and predict the behaviour of hackers. Firstly, there are frequent changes in hacker vocabulary, as discussed in relation to argot in Chapter 3, with differences in expressions that are used across different forums. Secondly, there is a lack of a ground truth data set. In the context of AI, ground truth refers to the labels assigned to the data sets used to train a machine learning model to link new inputs to outputs and to validate its performance (Lebovitz, Levina, & Lifshitz-Assaf, 2021). In other words, ground truth is information that is known to be real and true, as verified by direct observation and evidence. Achieving complete ground truth is a challenge in many areas but may be especially difficult in relation to hackers. After all, this is a population that is often driven to mask their identities and motivations. This is not a problem that is limited to machine learning. For instance, there are challenges in the media reporting of cybercrime and cyberwarfare (Lee, 2015), particularly around the verification of whether an incident happened and, if so, what exactly happened. It is also possible that AI is used in a defensive and offensive cybersecurity capacity by intelligence agencies and other government bodies but, not surprisingly, there is limited information available on such practices.

References

Adjerid, I., & Kelley, K. (2018). Big Data in Psychology: A Framework for Research Advancement. *American Psychologist, 73*(7), 899–917. doi:10.1037/amp0000190

Agassi, J., & Wiezenbaum, J. (1976). Computer Power and Human Reason: From Judgment to Calculation. *Technology and Culture, 17*, 813. doi:10.2307/3103715

Baki, S., Verma, R., Mukherjee, A., & Gnawali, O. (2017). *Scaling and Effectiveness of Email Masquerade Attacks: Exploiting Natural Language Generation*. Paper presented at the Proceedings of the 2017 ACM on Asia Conference on Computer and Communications Security, Abu Dhabi, United Arab Emirates. https://doi.org/10.1145/3052973.3053037

Bartoletti, M., Pes, B., & Serusi, S. (2018). *Data mining for detecting Bitcoin Ponzi schemes*. Paper presented at the Crypto Valley Conference on Blockchain Technology (CVCBT), Zug, Switzerland, Jun 20–22.

Benbouzid, B. (2019). To predict and to manage. Predictive policing in the United States. *Big Data & Society, 6*(1), 13. doi:10.1177/2053951719861703

Benjamin, V., Zhang, B., Nunamaker, J. F., & Chen, H. C. (2016). Examining hacker participation length in cybercriminal internet-relay-chat communities. *Journal of Management Information Systems, 33*(2), 482–510. doi:10.1080/07421222.2016.1205918

Browning, O. (2023). Boston Dynamics share compilation of robot 'working' on simulated job site. Retrieved from https://www.independent.co.uk/tv/lifestyle/building-job-robot-boston-dynamics-b2270529.html da Veiga, A., Astakhova, L. V., Botha, A., & Herselman, M. (2020). Defining organisational information security culture - Perspectives from academia and industry. *Computers & Security, 92*. doi:10.1016/j.cose.2020.101713

De Cosmo, L. (2022). Google Engineer Claims AI Chatbot Is Sentient: Why That Matters. *Scientific American,* July 12.

Dutta, S., Joyce, G., & Brewer, J. (2018). Utilizing chatbots to increase the efficacy of information security practitioners. In Nicholson, D. (Ed.), *Advances in Human Factors in Cybersecurity* (Vol. 593, pp. 237–243). Cham: Springer International Publishing Ag.

Grothaus, M. (2021). *Trust no one: inside the world of deepfakes.* London: Hodder Studio.

Guitton, M. J. (2020). Cybersecurity, social engineering, artificial intelligence, technological addictions: Societal challenges for the coming decade. *Comput. Hum. Behav., 107*(C), 2. doi:10.1016/j.chb.2020.106307

Guo, K. (2012). Holistic gaze strategy to categorize facial expression of varying intensities. *PLoS One, 7*(8), e42585. doi:10.1371/journal.pone.0042585

Heilweil, R. (2023). What is generative AI, and why is it suddenly everywhere? Retrieved from https://www.vox.com/recode/2023/1/5/23539055/generative-ai-chatgpt-stable-diffusion-lensa-dall-e

Jones, N. M., Wojcik, S. P., Sweeting, J., & Silver, R. C. (2016). Tweeting negative emotion: An investigation of Twitter data in the aftermath of violence on college campuses. *Psychological Methods, 21*(4), 526–541. doi:10.1037/met0000099

Kastrenakes. (2020). Google starts rolling out Duplex feature that can call salons to book a haircut for you: But nothing fancier than a basic haircut. Retrieved from https://www.theverge.com/2020/10/13/21514427/google-duplex-haircut-booking-feature-rolling-out-robot-natural-voice

Landers, R. N., Brusso, R. C., Cavanaugh, K. J., & Collmus, A. B. (2016). A primer on theory-driven web scraping: Automatic extraction of big data from the internet for use in psychological research. *Psychological Methods, 21*(4), 475–492. doi:10.1037/met0000081

Lebovitz, S., Levina, N., & Lifshitz-Assaf, H. (2021). Is AI Ground Truth Really True? The Dangers of Training and Evaluating AI Tools Based on Experts' Know-What. *MIS Quarterly, 45*, 1501–1526. doi:10.25300/MISQ/2021/16564

Lee, D. (2015). The daunting challenge of reporting on cyberwar. Retrieved from https://www.bbc.co.uk/news/technology-30813585

Li, X.-s., Fan, Z.-z., Ren, Y.-y., Zheng, X.-l., & Yang, R. (2021). Classification of Eye Movement and Its Application in Driving Based on a Refined Pre-Processing and Machine Learning Algorithm. *IEEE Access, PP*, 1. doi:10.1109/ACCESS.2021.3115961

Lima, A. Q., & Keegan, B. (2020).Challenges of using machine learning algorithms for cybersecurity: a study of threat-classification models applied to social media communication data. In Benson, V., & McAlaney, J. (Eds), *Cyber Influence and Cognitive Threats* (pp. 33–52). London: Academic Press.

Lippmann, R. P., Campbell, W. M., Weller-Fahy, D. J., Mensch, A. C., Zeno, G. M., & Campbell, J. P. (2016). *Finding Malicious Cyber Discussions in Social Media.* Retrieved from https://www.ll.mit.edu/sites/default/files/page/doc/2018-05/22_1_4_Campbell.pdf

Liu, Z., Tong, W., & Su, Y. (2020). Interaction effects of aging, word frequency, and predictability on saccade length in Chinese reading. *PeerJ, 8*, e8860. doi:10.7717/peerj.8860

Marin, E., Shakarian, J., & Shakarian, P. (2018). *Mining key-hackers on darkweb forums.* Paper presented at the 2018 1st International Conference on Data Intelligence and Security (ICDIS), 8–10 April.

Masling, J. M. (1966). Role-related behavior of the subject and psychologist and its effects upon psychological data. *Nebraska Symposium on Motivation, 14*, 67–103.

Muncaster, P. (2022). Experts Warn ChatGPT Could Democratize Cybercrime. Retrieved from https://www.infosecurity-magazine.com/news/experts-warn-chatgpt-democratize/

Nam, Y., Hong, U., Chung, H., & Noh, S. R. (2022). Eye Movement Patterns Reflecting Cybersickness: Evidence from Different Experience Modes of a Virtual Reality Game. *Cyberpsychol Behav Soc Netw, 25*(2), 135–139. doi:10.1089/cyber.2021.0167

Norman, K. L. (2017). *Cyberpsychology: an introduction to human-computer interaction* (second edition). Cambridge and New York: Cambridge University Press.

Nurse, J. R. C., Erola, A., Gibson-Robinson, T., Goldsmith, M., & Creese, S. (2016). Analytics for characterising and measuring the naturalness of online personae. *Security Informatics, 5*(1), 3. doi:10.1186/s13388-016-0028-1

Olson, P. (2012). *We Are Anonymous*. New York: Back Bay Books.

Orne, M. T. (1962). On the social psychology of the psychological experiment: With particular reference to demand characteristics and their implications [American Psychological Association doi:10.1037/h0043424]. Retrieved

Sample, I. (2020). What are deepfakes – and how can you spot them? Retrieved from https://www.theguardian.com/technology/2020/jan/13/what-are-deepfakes-and-how-can-you-spot-them

Shang, T., Lu, H., Wu, P., & Wei, Y. (2021). Eye-Tracking Evaluation of Exit Advance Guide Signs in Highway Tunnels in Familiar and Unfamiliar Drivers. *Int J Environ Res Public Health, 18*(13). doi:10.3390/ijerph18136820

Turing, A. M. (1950). Computing machinery and intelligence. *Mind, 49*, 433–460.

Vasek, M., & Moore, T. W. (2018). *Analyzing the Bitcoin Ponzi Scheme Ecosystem*. Paper presented at the Financial Cryptography Workshops.

Zhang, D., Liu, X., Xu, L., Li, Y., Xu, Y., Xia, M., . . . Wang, J. (2022). Effective differentiation between depressed patients and controls using discriminative eye movement features. *Journal of Affective Disorders, 307*, 237–243. doi:10.1016/j.jad.2022.03.077

Conclusions and recommendations

8

Opportunities and challenges in cybersecurity

Humans are complicated. Technology adds further unknowns in predicting behaviour by providing people with the ability to communicate in ways that have not previously been possible. This has created new opportunities and challenges, the extent of which are not fully understood. One way in which to approach this is perhaps to consider the fundamental question posed by Suler (2004) – does the internet enhance, or transform? Does the freedom and anonymity provided by the internet allow us to express ourselves more openly, or do we become a different person? This relates to the classification of cybercrime as being cyber-enabled or cyber-dependent. A cyber-enabled crime involves the individual using technology to commit a crime that could have also been committed offline, whereas cyber-dependent crimes are those which can only be committed by using technology. Hacking falls into the latter category, but it could be debated whether it really is a new behaviour. The stories of social engineers such as Jenny Radcliffe (Radcliffe, 2023) make it clear that gaining access to places was something they developed great skill at before the internet was widely available. Computer systems and the internet simply provide new spaces to explore.

Psychology research from both within and outside cybercrime can provide some insights into why people behave as they do when using socio-technical systems, and how harmful behaviours can be changed. It would be overly optimistic to say that psychology research can solve all the problems associated with cybercrime, but we would argue that there are significant benefits to be had from greater utilisation of psychological approaches in the prevention of

DOI: 10.4324/9781003300359-8

cybercrime. This would help facilitate a shift away from the view that humans are the weak link in cybersecurity, which is not a productive way of engaging with people to understand and change behaviour. Increasing the role of psychology in cybersecurity may also aide in prompting greater recognition and understanding of the risks of social engineering. Ethical social engineers can provide insight into how such criminal acts can be mitigated or prevented, but to date much of this understanding comes from media sources and personal accounts. We call for more empirical research that engages with ethical social engineers to develop an evidence base to improve cybersecurity practices. We argue that academic research is a strong position from which to follow this line of enquiry, due to the ethical standards to which we adhere and the experiences in disciplines such as psychology in investigating behaviors where there may be hesitancy on the part of study participants.

The motivations and techniques used by cybercriminals are diverse and linked to their sense of self-identity. The stereotype of a hacker as a teenage boy working from his mother's basement is inaccurate and counterproductive, as it can lead to assumptions that undermine prevention and intervention approaches. Hackers and cybercriminals are fully aware of these stereotypes and use the preconceptions that people have about them to obfuscate who they are and what their aims are. In keeping with a population that is so deeply immersed in internet culture, hackers are often also very self-aware of their perceived position in society, as expressed through discussions on hacking forums and self-referential jokes and memes. Nevertheless, for a population that seems to make an effort to portray itself as anarchistic and anti-social it is evident that socialisation and trust relationships are a key element of hacker activities. The role of hacking communities in providing people, including young people, with a sense of self-worth and social identity should not be underestimated, and of course once again the point must be made that being a hacker does not equate to be being a criminal.

The research on who is most likely to be a victim of different types of cybercrime is mixed. Given the breadth of different types of cybercrime, and the skill of attackers such as social engineers, it is difficult to envisage a situation where an organisation or any individual is completely free of any type of cyber-risk. As such it is important for individuals and organisations to develop resilience, in which they are able and supported to make positive adaptations after they have experienced a cyber-attack. Much of the research literature focusses on resilience at an organisational level, but there is potential to apply these concepts at the individual level as well. The victims of romance scams for example often report extensive feelings of shame for having fallen for the scam, and discussing concepts of resilience with such individuals may be an act of empowerment. It has been shown that the internet can enable those who have been the victim of a crime to express their experiences, such as in the #MeToo movement (Clark-Parsons, 2021). There are barriers and risks inherent in any online act, but the potential of the internet in enabling people to express their agency and respond, even indirectly, to those who have attacked them is worthy of further exploration.

The online environment also provides some unique opportunities for behaviour change and prevention strategies. This includes for example the monitoring of employee use of computer systems in the workplace, which provides the opportunity to deliver personalised, real-time behaviour change interventions. However, these possibilities also raise questions and debates on how such information is used, and whether individuals will be unfairly penalised for being a victim of a cybercrime. One of the recurrent themes throughout the book has been the surprising ease with which many cyber-attacks can be conducted, and the sophisticated psychological manipulations that social engineers and other attackers use to gain access to secure systems. Further, it could be argued that cybersecurity behaviour change and prevention strategies do not make full use of the extensive evidence base that is available from the psychology research literature. This does not mean of course that behaviour change and prevention strategies that have been successful in other domains should be assumed to be equally applicable to cybersecurity – the nature of the internet and the speed with which digital technologies evolve should make us cautious about such assumptions. This is why research is needed to understand the unique characteristics of digital technologies, and how these influence behaviour and decision making in cybersecurity. Behaviour change and prevention also need to be considered in relation not just to the targets of cybercrime, but also the instigators. Curiosity of computing systems and a desire to test the limits of what is possible appear to be the starting point for many of those who become involved in hacking, but these are not in themselves negative traits. Encouraging such individuals to work towards legitimate careers in cybersecurity can provide the resources and skills that will be needed if society is to be resilient against cybersecurity threats.

Recommendations for research, policy, and practice

Based on the research discussed in this book, the following recommendations are made:

- The concept of humans as the weak link in cybersecurity is not productive. If a system is repeatedly being breached due to actions that an individual is taking (such as clicking on a malicious link in a phishing email) then consideration needs to be given as to what it is about the design of that system that is facilitating the individual being influenced into taking the incorrect action. If for instance employees of an organisation in high-pressure roles are required to have complex passwords that are frequently changed then it should not come as a surprise to that organisation when employees start writing these passwords down.

- The manta of 'it's not if you get hacked, it's when you get hacked' serves a purpose of highlighting the risks of cyber-attack, but it also sends a message of it being futile to try to protect yourself. Awareness and education campaigns need to provide the target audience with practical advice and sources for support that demonstrate that cybersecurity threats can be avoided or at least mitigated through taking appropriate action.

- Given the high volume of cyber-attacks that organisations are subjected to, and the fact that attackers often only need one person in an organisation to engage with something like a phishing email for an attack to be selective, organisations need to create a culture where people feel they can safely report breaches. This type of organisational culture is partly set by the actions and statements of those in the leadership. For example, having a CEO disclose to employees that they themselves fell for a phishing email – but then quickly notified IT when they had realised their mistake – would help create an organisational culture that supports reporting of cyber-risks.

- Whilst allowing for the fact that it is impossible to completely prevent any cyber-attacks from occurring it is also the case that many large, well-funded organisations continue to be the victim of cyber-attacks due to very basic gaps in their security. This is something that is frequently a cause of frustration for those in the hacking community, who feel that these organisations should be putting more effort into protecting their systems. This is particularly the case when the organisation holds data about members of the public. There is a need for organisations to understand the seriousness of cyber-risks, and to prioritise resources appropriately. It is telling that the Chief Technology Officer (typically the most senior person directly responsible for cybersecurity) is often not included on the Board of Directors of large organisations.

- It is important to promote the concept of resilience, and to support individuals and organisations to develop relevant skills that empower them to adapt to any cybersecurity incident they experience in a way that will help lead to a more positive outcome in any future incidents.

- Young people and others with an interest in hacking should be encouraged to develop these skills in a safe and legal way. There are legitimate resources available to support this, although at present there remain negative connotations about hacking, in which it is often assumed to be a criminal activity. This would help address the cybersecurity recruitment crisis, which refers to the lack of trained and qualified cybersecurity practitioners that has been documented in many countries.

- There is a need for greater awareness of social engineering, which can be achieved through education and training campaigns in public and organisational settings. We would note that stories and examples of social engineering attacks can often be entertaining and of interest to people, as evidenced by popular books such as *People Hacker: Confessions of a Burglar for Hire* by Jenny Radcliffe (2023). As such educating people about social engineering may be an easier task than attempting to engage with them on the more technical aspects of cybersecurity.

- Prevention, harm reduction, and behaviour change campaigns can be challenging to implement but can also be successful. It is vital however that any such campaigns are based on evidence from the research literature. Care should be taken not to implement for example a behaviour change technique just because it intuitively feels that it will be effective. Fear appeals for instance may be effective in some contexts, but in others may have the unintended consequence of causing employees to conclude that there is nothing they can do to avoid a cyber-attack, and therefore there is no point in even trying. In other words, behaviour change by itself is not necessarily that difficult – it is changing the behaviour in the desired direction that is the hard part.

References

Byford, K. S. (1998). Privacy in Cyberspace: Constructing a Model of Privacy for the Electronic Communications Environment. *Rutgers Computer and Technology Law Journal, 24*, 1–74.

Clark-Parsons, R. (2021). "I SEE YOU, I BELIEVE YOU, I STAND WITH YOU": #MeToo and the performance of networked feminist visibility. *Feminist Media Studies, 21*(3), 362–380. doi:10.1080/14680777.2019.1628797

Radcliffe, J. (2023). *People Hacker: Confessions of a Burglar for Hire*. London: Simon & Schuster.

Suler, J. (2004). The online disinhibition effect. *Cyberpsychology & Behaviour, 7*(3), 321–326. doi:10.1089/1094931041291295

Glossary

Artificial intelligence (AI)   Computer systems that can perform tasks normally requiring human intelligence, such as visual perception, decision-making, and participating in conversations in a meaningful way.

Big data   Data of such size and complexity that it cannot be analysed using conventional means, such as the vast amounts of data generated every day by social media platforms.

Black/ grey/ white hat   Terms used to indicate the motivations and boundaries of hackers, from those who are criminals who will break into and/ or damage a computer system with malicious intent (black hat); those who will test computer systems for legitimate and ethical reasons (white hat); and those who combine both legitimate and illegitimate practices (grey hat).

Botnet   A group of internet-connected devices that is used, often without the knowledge of the device owners, by attackers to carry out powerful attacks by cyber-adversaries such as the execution of a **DDoS** attack.

CaaS (Crimeware-as-a-Service)   A criminal business model in which cyber-criminals provide their knowledge, services, infrastructures, and software tools to other criminals for a fee.

Cryptocurrency   Decentralised digital currency that can be used as a form of payment online, usually with a greater degree of anonymity than in traditional currencies. One of the most well-known cryptocurrencies is Bitcoin.

Cyberwarfare   Using hacking and/ or social engineering approaches to cause harm and disruption amongst a population. This can include the creation and dissemination of **fake news.**

Dark web   Internet content that can only be accessed using specialised software such as **Tor**. Often associated with criminality but can also be used for legitimate purposes such as communication by journalists reporting from oppressive regimes. This is distinct from the **deep web.**

Data mining   The process of sorting through **big data** sets to identify patterns and relationships, which utilises techniques from **machine learning**.

DDoS (Distributed Denial of Service)   A type of cyber-attack in which the targeted computer system is overwhelmed and made inoperable by a high volume of internet requests, akin to attempting to refresh a webpage many thousands of times per section. Often achieved through use of a **botnet.**

Deepfake   Fake but highly realistic images or videos created with the use of **artificial intelligence**. Often used as part of a scam or act of **cyberwarfare**.

Deep web   Internet content that cannot be located or accessed using standard search engines, such as for example online databases containing medical records or school grades. This is distinct from the **dark web.**

Fake news   False or misleading information that is presented as fact, created, and disseminated with the intention of causing disruption, changing behaviour, shaping beliefs, or generating profit through advertising revenue. Often used as a tool for **cyberwarfare.**

Hacker   An individual with knowledge of information technology and the skills necessary to use, and potentially change, a computer system to achieve a goal or overcome a challenge. Often this is conflated with criminal intent.

Insider threat   The threat caused by the actions of a member of an organisation that either facilitates or causes a cybersecurity incident. This can be in the form of an unintentional insider threat (e.g., an employee clicking on a malicious link in a phishing email) or intentional insider threat (e.g., an employee deliberately stealing company secrets and selling these to a competitor).

Machine learning (ML)   A branch of **artificial intelligence** that involves using data and algorithms to imitate how humans learn, with the goal of improving accuracy over time.

Malware   Malicious software that is intentionally designed to cause harm to a computer system, including by accessing sensitive data.

Penetration testing   A simulated cyber-attack on an organisation that helps that organisation understand the gaps and weaknesses in their defences.

Phishing email   An email that attempts to trick or scam the receiver into performing an action that will facilitate a cyber-breach, such as disclosing sensitive information or clicking on a malicious link/ attachment that will install **malware** and compromise the targeted computer system.

Phishing website   A website designed to collect sensitive information from a target, which may also infect the target's device with **malware**. Often these sites will be set up to resemble a genuine and well-known website, such as a major social media platform.

Ransomeware Malicious software that is designed to encrypt the data held by an organisation, preventing that organisation from accessing their own data until a ransom is paid and the attackers provide the decryption key.

Script-kiddie A type of **hacker** who relies on software written by others to hack. Such an individual may be lacking in a fundamental understanding of the technologies they are using to enable their hacking activities.

Server A computer program or device that provides a service to other computers or their users, such as for example a bank server that operates the software and systems that the staff of that bank use for their daily work activities.

Spear-phishing A **phishing email** that is specifically targeted at an individual or individuals, such as the senior management of a company.

Tor (The Onion Router) Open source and free software that enables anonymous internet communication. Often used in association with the **dark web.**

Virtual Private Network (VPN) Software that protects users by encrypting their data and masks the physical location of the device being used.

Index

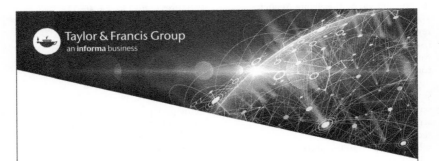

For Product Safety Concerns and Information please contact our EU
representative GPSR@taylorandfrancis.com Taylor & Francis Verlag GmbH,
Kaufingerstraße 24, 80331 München, Germany

Printed and bound by CPI Group (UK) Ltd, Croydon, CR0 4YY
08/06/2025
01897009-0012